T0150967

STAN TEKIELA's

Birding for
Beginners

Northeast

**Your Guide to Feeders, Food
and the Most Common Backyard Birds**

by Stan Tekiela

Adventure Publications
Cambridge, Minnesota

DEDICATION

To the memory of my mother, Adele.

Edited by Brett Ortler and Dan Downing

Cover, book design and illustrations by Jonathan Norberg

Cover photos by Stan Tekiela. Front: Baltimore Oriole **Back:** White-breasted Nuthatch
All photos by Stan Tekiela except pg. 20 (Barn Swallow) by **Mirko Graul/Shutterstock**; pg. 20 (Northern Flicker) by **Anatoliy Lukich/Shutterstock**; pg. 19 (Ruby-throated Hummingbird) by **Gerald Marella/Shutterstock**; pg. 142 (displaying) by **Hartmut Walter**; pg. 148 (juvenile) by **Brian K. Wheeler** and pg. 144 (main) by **Jim Zipp**

To the best of the publisher's knowledge, all photos were of live birds. Some were photographed in a controlled condition.

10 9 8 7 6 5 4 3

Stan Tekiela's Birding for Beginners: Northeast
First Edition 2020
Copyright © 2020 by Stan Tekiela
Published by Adventure Publications
An imprint of AdventureKEEN
310 Garfield Street South
Cambridge, Minnesota 55008
(800) 678-7006
www.adventurepublications.net
All rights reserved
Printed in the United States of America
ISBN 978-1-64755-118-6 (pbk.); ISBN 978-1-64755-119-3 (ebook)

Table of Contents

INTRODUCTION

THE BIRDS

Getting Started

Welcome to the world of birding! If you're a beginner trying to identify the birds in your backyard, this book is for you. Birding is a simple pastime that's incredibly popular, and it's not hard to see why: You can watch birds in any season, and as far as hobbies go, a basic setup is about as cheap as it gets. All you need is some green space, a bird feeder and perhaps a pair of binoculars. I've written this book to help birders who are just starting out. This book contains 54 species of birds in the Northeast, all common backyard visitors. It includes summertime favorites such as orioles, bluebirds and the Ruby-throated Hummingbird and year-round residents such as cardinals, chickadees and nuthatches. The birds I chose for this book are among the most common and familiar visitors to backyard feeders.

Once you start identifying backyard birds, I'd encourage you to find my state-specific field guide for your state. I've written guides for nearly every state in the Northeast, and each book contains around 120 species, including a wide variety of birds you're not as likely to spot in an average backyard, including raptors, shorebirds and more. It also contains a detailed range map for each species, showing when and where each bird is usually found.

I sincerely hope you enjoy your start to bird watching. Have fun, and again, welcome!

Baltimore Oriole male

Bird Feeder Basics

To get more birds to visit your yard, an easy way to invite them is to put out bird feeders. Bird feeders are often as unique as the birds themselves, so the types of feeders you use really depends on the kinds of birds you're trying to attract.

Hopper feeders are often wooden or plastic. Designed to hold a large amount of seeds, they often have a slender opening along the bottom, which dispenses the seeds. Birds land along the sides and help themselves to the food. Hopper feeders work well as main feeders in conjunction with other types of feeders. They are perfect for offering several kinds of seed mixes for cardinals, finches, nuthatches, chickadees and more.

Tube feeders with large seed ports and multiple perches are very popular. Often mostly plastic, they tend to be rugged enough to last several years and can be easily cleaned. These feeders are great for black oil sunflower seeds and seed mixes, which are favorites of grosbeaks and all the other bird species that also visit hopper feeders.

Some tube feeders have small holes, allowing incredibly tiny thistle seeds

to be dispensed just a few at a time. Use this kind of feeder to offer Nyjer seed, which will attract various finches.

Other styles of tube feeders have a wire mesh covering with openings large enough for birds to extract one of their favorite foods—peanuts out of the shell. Most birds enjoy peanuts, so these feeders will be some of the most popular in your yard. Another variety of tube feeder has openings large enough for peanuts in the shell. These are also very popular with the birds.

Ground feeders allow a wide variety of birds to access the food. The simplest and easiest feeders to use, they consist of a flat platform with a lip around the edges to keep seeds from spilling out. Some have a roof to keep rain and snow off the food. With or without a roof, drainage holes in the bottom are important. Ground feeders will bring in juncos and many other birds to your backyard, including pheasants, and even mallards if you're near water.

Suet feeders are simply wire cages that hold cakes of suet. The wire allows woodpeckers, nuthatches and other birds to cling securely to the feeder while pecking out chunks of suet. The best suet feeders have a vertical extension at the bottom where a woodpecker can brace its tail and support itself while feeding. These are called tail-prop suet feeders.

Nectar feeders are glass or plastic containers that hold sugar water. These feeders usually have plastic parts that are bright red, a color that is extremely attractive to hummingbirds, but orioles and woodpeckers will also stop for a drink. They often have up to four ports for access to the liquid and yellow bee guards to prevent bees from getting inside.

Mealworm feeders can be very basic—a simple glass or plastic cup or container will do. Pick one with sides tall enough and make sure the material is slippery enough to stop the lively mealworms from crawling out. Bluebirds especially love this wiggly treat!

Get to Know Your Birdseed

 **Black Oil Sunflower:** Studies have shown that all birds prefer black oil sunflower seeds over all other commercial bird foods. Black oilers are smooth black seeds that come from the common sunflower plant, *Helianthus annuus*. Even smaller birds such as finches have no trouble cracking open these seeds with their large, strong bills.

Black oilers contain more fat in the form of oil than other seeds, hence the name. They are meatier and pack more nourishment per bite than just about any other bird food on the market. Each seed has a nutritional value of 28% fat, 15% protein and 25% fiber and supplies vitamins B and E as well as calcium, iron and potassium.

 **Striped Sunflower:** Striped sunflower seeds have a thin white stripe. They are larger than black oilers, and they have a thicker hull, making them harder to split. Nevertheless, Blue Jays open them easily and like them immensely. Occasionally called stripers, these are the sunflower seeds that people eat. High in fat, protein, vitamins and fiber, they are usually a part of any popular birdseed mix.

 **White Safflower:** This is a good option for those who want to avoid attracting squirrels and grackles, which often find it distasteful and difficult to open. It attracts many backyard favorites, such as cardinals, chickadees and more. Smaller than black oil seed, safflower is a thick-shelled, small white seed that is high in nutrition and fat. These seeds come from the annual safflower plant, *Carthamus tinctorius*.

Golden Safflower: Enjoyed by nuthatches, cardinals and other strong-billed birds, this is an improved variety of white safflower that is also called NutraSaff safflower. Introduced in 2004, it has a thinner outer hull, high oil content, high protein and polyunsaturated omega-6 fatty acids. Developed as food for beef and dairy cattle, poultry and fish and for bird feed markets.

Hulled Sunflower: Hulled sunflower is just the meat (or nutmeat) of the sunflower seed without the hard, inedible outer shell. The nutritional content is the same as black oil and striped sunflower seeds. There is no possibility for these seeds to germinate, so the bags are marketed as "non-germinating" or "no-mess" mixes. With hulled sunflower, you won't need to rake up or blow away discarded hulls under your feeders.

Hulled sunflower is often available as whole nuts or as pieces or chips. The expense of shelling the seeds makes this feed more expensive than others, but the benefits may outweigh the cost. After all, most birdseed is sold by weight, and with hulled sunflower you are not paying for the inedible shells.

White Millet: Millet is a soft-shelled, small round grain that comes from the millet plant, *Panicum milieaceum*. There are red, golden and striped varieties of millet, but the most common for bird feeding is proso millet, which is white.

White millet attracts a variety of birds, including sparrows, juncos and doves. It contains good nutritional content: around 4% fat, 12% protein and 8% fiber, vitamin B and calcium. An affordable seed that is usually offered in ground and tray feeders, it is also sprinkled on the ground to attract birds to the feeders.

 **Cracked Corn:** At a wonderful low cost, cracked corn is a great option to feed large numbers of wild birds on the ground. It also attracts rabbits, squirrels, raccoons and opossums. Offerings of cracked corn will keep the squirrels busy with something to eat, keeping them from your feeders filled with the higher-priced foods for the birds.

Cracked corn is exactly what it sounds like—dried whole corn kernels that have been cracked open. There can be a lot of dust associated with cracked corn, but it's worth it. This food won't sprout and grow in your garden or lawn, and birds/squirrels eat everything, so there's no waste. Low in fat but high in protein and fiber, it is often a base in bird food blends. Offer it in large open-tray, fly-through or ground feeders or sprinkle it around on the ground.

 **Whole Corn:** Whole corn consists of unbroken kernels of dried corn and is often part of the base of wild bird food mixes. It is less desirable to birds than cracked corn and usually is thought of as wildlife food since it attracts squirrels, chipmunks, raccoons, opossums and other animals. You can offer it in a large tray or trough ground feeder or spread it on the ground.

 **Peanuts:** Peanuts are another option to feed birds. The peanut plant, *Arachis hypogaea*, is a member of the legume or bean family and the peanuts grow underground. Peanuts contain about 45% fat and 24% protein, and they are a good source of vitamins A and E as well as zinc, iron and potassium.

Peanut pieces are popular in seed mixes and suet. Many birds will eat them in any form—shelled, in small chips or whole in the shell. They gobble up peanuts quickly, so sprinkle them with a feed mix or place them in a feeder with a tight mesh to prevent large amounts from spilling out all at once.

You can also try offering peanuts in the shell to birds. Put them in a larger mesh feeder with large openings so the birds can extract the entire nut. Peanuts get wet and tend to mold, so avoid putting out a lot at one time.

MIXES

Songbird Mix: Just about every major retailer has its own version of a songbird mix. It is often a combination of black oil sunflower seeds, striped sunflower seeds, safflower, cracked corn and other ingredients. The amount and proportion of seeds vary from store to store, but the main seed in these mixes are black oil seeds. To start getting familiar songbirds to come to your yard, offer a songbird mix.

Premium or Deluxe Blend: Premium blends are often a base of black oil sunflower seeds combined with striped sunflower seeds and safflower. The addition of peanuts, shelled or whole, upgrades any regular blend to premium or deluxe. Sometimes these mixtures also contain raisins, cranberries or other dried fruit. All sorts of birds love this rich food, and it is great for winter when you want to offer an extra-special treat.

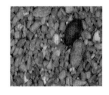

Non-germinating Mix: Non-germinating mixes are composed of seeds that have been removed from their shells. Because seeds without shells will not germinate, people who don't want rogue sunflowers growing in their lawns or gardens may want to try it.

These mixes often have 2–3 varieties of seeds, with whole nuts or pieces of seed meat. Non-germinating may look like the most expensive seed per pound, but you're not paying for hulls, which are included in the weight of other seeds but aren't eaten.

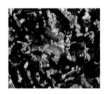

Specialty Mix: Many seed stores make a specialty blend that is unique to their store and works well for their region. In the Northeast, black oil sunflower seed is the main ingredient. Stores may also mix more striped sunflower seeds, safflower, peanuts or cracked or whole corn with seeds.

Other Foods

Suet: Another way to attract birds, especially woodpeckers, is to offer suet. Suet cakes are composed mainly of beef fat. Specifically, it is cow fat from around the kidneys and loins. However, more and more suet is coming from cow fat anywhere on the animal.

Suet is an extremely high-energy food with a high calorie count, and many birds can easily digest it. Some varieties are mixed with seeds, nuts or dried fruit. Suet in these forms is a great way to give your backyard birds an especially tasty treat.

Offer suet in specialized wire feeders with a bottom perch. These allow birds to reach in to the cake and break off small pieces. Hang your suet feeders in areas where squirrels, chipmunks, raccoons and opossums will have trouble accessing them, otherwise, they will take the entire cake.

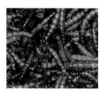

Mealworms: Mealworms are the worm-like larvae of darkling beetles, which are flightless insects. An excellent source of protein, calcium and vitamins, the offering of mealworms will attract bluebirds, as well as a variety of birds that don't normally come to traditional seed feeders.

Mealworms can be purchased live or dried. Both are sold in large quantities, and for good reason. When birds find them, they gorge themselves. Live mealworms must be stored in a container from which they cannot escape. A steep container with slippery sides is essential, and it should be refrigerated. Offer dried mealworms in a shallow tray.

Fresh & Dried Fruit: Offering fresh fruit, such as orange halves, is a popular way to bring in orioles and other popular birds. Many fresh fruits, including bananas, apples, melons and grapes, and dried fruits, such as raisins, currants and prunes, are good choices to put out.

Orioles will come to orange halves placed sunny-side up and impaled on a nail to secure them. Fresh fruit slices can become messy and attract insects and mammals. To keep animals away, provide the fruit on a platform with a squirrel or raccoon baffle.

Grape Jelly: Orioles and other birds also like the sweet taste of grape jelly. They will come to this highly sugared, high-energy food early in spring when the weather can be cold and wet. Many types of commercial jelly feeders are available, but you can offer the treat in a small tray, cup or other container. To prevent the birds from getting jelly on their feathers, offer small portions each time.

Peanut Butter: Regular smooth or chunky peanut butter is another good food to attract a wide variety of birds to your yard. Offer it like suet in specialized feeders or just smear it on a chunk of bark, directly onto a tree or on a suet cake. You can offer this high-energy food in your own creative ways. However you present it, birds will quickly find it.

Storing Birdseed and Feeder Maintenance

Storing birdseed safely is easy. Keep it out of the house, preferably in a cool, dry place away from direct sunlight. Garages and sheds are the best places to stow feed since the cooler temperatures there will reduce the number of grain moths hatching out of the seeds.

Transfer seed out of its original plastic or paper bag into a clean container. The container should be upright, semi-airtight and prevent mice, chipmunks and other rodents from chewing through and getting to the seed. Metal garbage cans are good choices for storage. Use several to store different kinds of food.

Try to avoid buying bird food in very large quantities. Pick up just enough to feed birds for a month or so. Make sure you use up the oldest seed before opening your more recent purchases.

Always try to use rubber gloves when handling your feeders and cleaning the feeding area because there are several diseases that can be picked up from bird droppings. Histoplasmosis is a disease caused by breathing in *Histoplasma capsulatum*, a fungus in soils that comes from bird and bat droppings. It is recommended to wear a particulate mask while raking up or blowing away seed hulls underneath feeders. Many people who contract histoplasmosis don't develop symptoms, but some exhibit mild flu-like symptoms and, rarely, serious complications.

Cryptococcosis is another fungal disease found in the environment, and it also comes from bird droppings. Often associated with pigeon droppings, it is best to wear rubber gloves and a mask when cleaning up scat on feeders and around roosting sites, attics, cupolas and other places where large numbers of birds gather. Like histoplasmosis, many people don't suffer any symptoms, and some come down with mild flu-like symptoms.

West Nile virus is carried by mosquitoes. Crows, jays and other birds contract it but don't transfer it to humans, so there is no need to be concerned about getting this disease from your feeders.

Keeping your feeding station clean and refreshing the site are quick and easy ways to stop the spread of avian disease and other diseases from bird droppings.

What's That Bird? Tips for Identifying Birds

Identifying birds isn't as difficult as you might think. By simply following a few basic strategies, you can increase your chances of successfully identifying most birds that you see. One of the first and easiest things to do when you see a new bird is to note its **color**. This field guide is organized by color, so simply turn to the right color section to find it.

House Sparrow

American Robin

American Crow

Canada Goose

Next, note the **size of the bird.** A strategy to quickly estimate size is to compare different birds. Pick a small, a medium and a large bird. Select an American Robin as the medium bird. Measured from bill tip to tail tip, a robin is 10 inches (25 cm). Now select two other birds, one smaller and one larger. Good choices are a House Sparrow, at about 6 inches (15 cm), and an American Crow, around 18 inches (45 cm). When you see a species you don't know, you can now quickly ask yourself, "Is it larger than a sparrow but smaller than a robin?" When you look in your field guide to identify your bird, you would check the species that are roughly 6–10 inches (15–25 cm). This will help to narrow your choices.

Ruby-throated Hummingbird

Northern Cardinal

Hairy Woodpecker

Cooper's Hawk

Next, note the **size, shape and color of the bill.** Is it long or short, thick or thin, pointed or blunt, curved or straight? Seed-eating birds, such as cardinals, have bills that are thick and strong enough to crack even the toughest seeds. Birds that sip nectar, such as Ruby-throated Hummingbirds, need long, thin bills to reach deep into flowers. Hawks and owls tear their prey with very sharp, curving bills. Sometimes, just noting the bill shape can help you decide whether the bird is a woodpecker, finch, grosbeak, blackbird or bird of prey.

Northern Flicker

Noticing **what the bird is eating** will give you another clue to help you identify the species. Feeding is a big part of any bird's life. Fully one-third of all bird activity revolves around searching for food, catching prey and eating. While birds don't always follow all the rules of their diet, you can make some general assumptions. Northern Flickers, for instance, feed on ants and other insects, so you wouldn't expect to see them visiting a seed feeder. Other birds, such as Barn and Tree Swallows, eat flying insects and spend hours swooping and diving to catch a meal.

Barn Swallow

Birds in flight are harder to identify, but noting the **wing size and shape** will help. Wing size is in direct proportion to body size, weight and type of flight. Wing shape determines whether the bird flies fast and with precision, or slowly and less precisely. Barn Swallows, for instance, have short, pointed wings that slice through the air, enabling swift, accurate flight. House Finches have short, rounded wings, helping them to flit through thick tangles of branches.

Some bird species have a unique **pattern of flight** that can help in identification. Pileated Woodpeckers fly in a distinctive undulating pattern (next page) that makes it look like they're riding a roller coaster.

While it's not easy to make all of these observations in the short time you often have to watch a "mystery" bird, practicing these identification methods will greatly expand your birding skills. To further improve your skills, seek the guidance of a more experienced birder who can answer your questions on the spot.

Bird Basics

It's easier to identify birds and communicate about them if you know the names of the different parts of a bird. For instance, it's more effective to use the word "crest" to indicate the set of extra-long feathers on top of a Northern Cardinal's head than to try to describe it. The following illustration points out the basic parts of a bird. Because it is a composite of many birds, it shouldn't be confused with any actual bird.

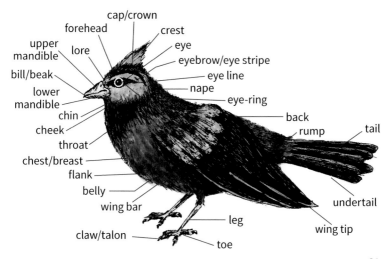

Indigo Buntings: female, male

BIRD COLOR VARIABLES

No other animal has a color palette like birds. Brilliant blues, lemon yellows, showy reds and iridescent greens are common in the bird world. In general, male birds are more colorful than their female counterparts. This helps males attract a mate, essentially saying, "Hey, look at me!" Color calls attention to a male's health as well. The better the condition of his feathers, the better his food source, territory and potential for mating.

When male and female birds of the same species don't look like each other, they are called sexually dimorphic, meaning "two forms." Dimorphic females often have a nondescript, dull color, as seen in Indigo Buntings. Muted tones not only help females hide during the weeks of motionless incubation but also draw less attention to them when they're out feeding or taking a break from the rigors of raising the young.

The males and females of some species, such as the Downy Woodpecker, Blue Jay and Bald Eagle, look nearly identical. In woodpeckers, they are differentiated by only a red (sometimes yellow or black) mark; this mark may be on top of the head, on the face or nape, or just behind the bill.

During the first year, juvenile birds often look like their mothers. Since brightly colored feathers are used mainly for attracting a mate, young non-breeding males don't have a need for colorful plumage. It's not until the first spring molt (or several years later, depending on the species) that young males obtain their breeding colors.

Both breeding and winter plumages are the result of molting. Molting is the process of dropping old, worn feathers and replacing them with new ones. All birds molt, typically twice a year, with the spring molt usually occurring in late winter. At this time, most birds produce their brighter breeding plumage, which lasts throughout the summer.

American Goldfinch winter plumage

Winter plumage is the result of the late-summer molt, which serves a couple of important functions. First, it adds feathers for warmth in the coming winter season. Second, in some species it produces feathers that tend to be drab in color, which helps to camouflage the birds and hide them from predators. The winter plumage of the male American Goldfinch, for example, is olive brown, unlike its canary-yellow breeding color during summer. Luckily for us, some birds, such as the male Northern Cardinal, retain their bright summer colors all year long.

BIRD NESTS

Bird nests are a true feat of engineering. Imagine constructing a home that's strong enough to weather storms, large enough to hold your entire family, insulated enough to shelter them from cold and

Northern Cardinal

heat, and waterproof enough to keep out rain. Think about building it without blueprints or directions and using mainly your feet. Birds do this!

Before building, birds must select an appropriate site. In some species, such as the House Wren, the male picks out several potential sites and assembles small twigs in each. The "extra" nests, called dummy nests, discourage other birds from using any nearby cavities for their nests. The male takes the female around and shows her the choices. After choosing her favorite, she finishes the construction.

In other species, such as the Baltimore Oriole, the female selects the site and builds the nest, while the male offers an occasional suggestion. Each bird species has its own nest-building routine that is strictly followed.

As you can see in the photos on pp. 25–27, birds build a wide variety of nests.

Nesting material often consists of natural items found in the immediate area. Most nests consist of plant fibers (such as bark from grapevines), sticks, mud, dried grass, feathers, fur or soft, fuzzy tufts from thistle. Some birds, including Ruby-throated Hummingbirds, use spiderwebs to glue nest materials together.

Transportation of nesting material is limited to the amount a bird can hold or carry. Birds must make many trips afield to gather enough material to complete a nest. Most nests take four days or more, and hundreds, if not thousands, of trips to build.

Canada Goose nest

A **ground nest** can be a mound of vegetation on the ground or in the water. It can also be just a simple, shallow depression scraped out in earth, stones or sand. Killdeer scrape out ground nests without adding any nesting material.

Double-crested Cormorant nest

The **platform nest** represents a much more complex type of construction. Typically built with twigs or sticks and branches, this nest forms a platform and has a depression in the center to nestle the eggs. Platform nests can be in trees; on balconies, cliffs, bridges or man-made platforms; and even in flowerpots. They often provide space for the adventurous young and function as a landing platform for the parents.

Mourning Doves and herons don't anchor their platform nests to trees, so these can tumble from branches during high winds and storms. Hawks, eagles, ospreys and other birds construct sturdier platform nests with large sticks and branches.

Other platform nests are constructed on the ground with mud, grass and other vegetation from the area. Many waterfowl build platform nests on the ground near or in water. A **floating platform nest** moves with the water level, preventing the nest, eggs and birds from being flooded.

Northern Cardinal nest

Three-quarters of all songbirds construct a **cup nest,** which is a modified platform nest. The supporting platform is built first and attached firmly to a tree, shrub or rock ledge, or it is built on the ground. Next, the sides are constructed with grass, small twigs, bark or leaves, which are woven together and often glued with mud for added strength. The inner cup is contoured last and can be lined with down feathers, animal fur or hair, or soft plant materials.

The **pendulous nest** is an unusual nest that looks like a sock hanging from a branch. Attached to the end of small branches of trees, this unique nest is inaccessible to most predators and often waves wildly in a breeze.

Baltimore Oriole nest

Woven tightly with plant fibers, the pendulous nest is strong and watertight and takes up to a week to build. A small opening at the top or on the side allows parents access to the grass-lined interior. More commonly used by tropical birds, this complex nest has also been mastered by orioles and kinglets. It must be one heck of a ride to be inside one of these nests during a windy spring thunderstorm!

The **cavity nest** is used by many species of birds, most notably woodpeckers and Eastern Bluebirds. A cavity nest is often excavated from a branch or tree trunk and offers shelter from storms, sun, cold and predators. A small entrance hole in a tree can lead to a nest chamber that is up to a safe 10 inches (25 cm) deep.

Red-bellied Woodpecker nest

Typically made by woodpeckers, cavity nests are usually used only once by the builder. Nest cavities can be used for many subsequent years by inhabitants such as Tree Swallows, mergansers and bluebirds. Kingfishers, on the other hand, can dig a tunnel up to 4 feet (1 m) long into a riverbank. The nest chamber at the end of the tunnel is already well insulated, so it's usually only sparsely lined.

Indigo Bunting nest with Brown-headed Cowbird egg (speckled)

One of the most clever of all nests is the **no nest,** or daycare nest. Parasitic birds, such as Brown-headed Cowbirds, don't build their own nests. Instead, the egg-laden female searches out the nest of another bird and sneaks in to lay an egg while the host mother isn't looking.

A mother cowbird wastes no energy building a nest only to have it raided by a predator. Laying her eggs in the nests of other birds transfers the responsibility of raising her young to the host. When she lays her eggs in several nests, the chances increase that at least one of her babies will live to maturity.

WHO BUILDS THE NEST?

Generally, the female bird constructs the nest. She gathers the materials and does the building, with an occasional visit from her mate to check on progress. In some species, both parents contribute equally. The male may forage for sticks, grass or mud, but the female often fashions the nest. Only rarely does a male build a nest by himself.

WHY BIRDS MIGRATE

Why do so many species of birds migrate? The short answer is simple: food. Birds migrate to locations with abundant food, as it is easier to breed where there is food than where food is scarce. Scarlet Tanagers, for instance, are **complete migrators** that fly from the tropics of South America to nest in the forests of North America, where billions of newly hatched insects are available to feed to their young.

Other migrators, such as some birds of prey, migrate back to northern regions in spring. In these locations, they hunt mice, voles and other small rodents that are beginning to breed.

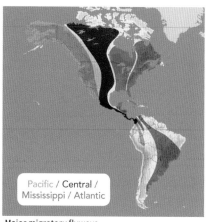

Pacific / **Central** / Mississippi / Atlantic

Major migratory flyways

Complete migrators have a set time and pattern of migration. Every year at nearly the same time, they head to a specific wintering ground. Complete migrators may travel great distances, sometimes 15,000 miles (24,100 km) or more in one year.

Complete migration doesn't necessarily mean flying from Ohio to a tropical destination. Dark-eyed Juncos, for example, are complete migrators that move from the far reaches of Canada to spend the winter here in the cold and snowy Northeast. This trip is still considered complete migration.

Complete migrators have many interesting aspects. In spring, males often leave a few weeks before the females, arriving early to scope

Dark-eyed Junco female

out possibilities for nesting sites and food sources and to begin to defend territories. The females arrive several weeks later. In many species, the females and their young leave earlier in the fall, often up to four weeks before the adult males.

Other species, such as the American Goldfinch, are **partial migrators.** These birds usually wait until their food supplies dwindle before flying south. Unlike complete migrators, partial migrators move only far enough south, or sometimes east and west, to find abundant food. In some years it might be only a few hundred miles, while in other years it can be as many as a

American Goldfinch male

thousand. This kind of migration, dependent on weather and the availability of food, is sometimes called seasonal movement.

Unlike the predictable complete migrators or partial migrators, **irruptive migrators** may move every third to fifth year or, in some cases, in consecutive years. These migrations are triggered when times are tough and food is scarce. Red-breasted Nuthatches are irruptive migrators. They leave their normal northern range in search of more food or in response to overpopulation.

Many other birds don't migrate at all. Black-capped Chickadees, for example, are **non-migrators** that remain in their habitat all year long and only move around as necessary to find food.

Tips for a Bird-Friendly Yard

Plant native plants—a green lawn looks pretty, but it doesn't offer all that much for birds or other wildlife. A yard full of native or other flowering plants, on the other hand, is like putting out the welcome mat for birds, especially when those plants offer cover (think shrubs/bushes), food sources (native and non-native cultivated plants, wildflowers or fruit-bearing trees) or nesting materials or sites. And you don't need a huge space to help the birds: Even a container garden with native plants can help!

Avoid insecticides, herbicides and other chemical treatments. Many birds depend on insects as a major part of their diet, and the same is true of weed seeds. Most insecticides on the market are broad-spectrum, which means they kill the bugs you're targeting (mosquitoes!) but many other insects that too, including bees, butterflies and the like.

Provide bird food consistently, along with water. Consistency is key when it comes to bird feeding. If you only happen to put out birdseed once in a while, you'll attract fewer birds than if you do so regularly. Choose high-quality birdseed, and offer a variety of foods, if possible. When you're putting out bird food, provide a birdbath too. Don't feed birds if your feeder potentially puts birds in danger (e.g., where a window strike could happen or near a busy road).

Downy Woodpecker

Keep cats indoors. Cats are a major threat to birds and other wildlife. If you have a house cat, keep it indoors.

Do-it-Yourself Bird Food

A BASIC PEANUT BUTTER SPREAD FOR BIRDS

Ingredients:
½ cup raisins
½ cup granola
½ cup oatmeal
½ cup Cheerios
16-ounce jar smooth peanut butter

Directions: Mix dry ingredients in a large mixing bowl. Warm the peanut butter in a microwave or place the jar in warm water to soften. Scoop out the softened peanut butter, and mix it well with the dry ingredients until smooth.

Spread on tree bark or smear a few dollops on the tray of a feeder.

A SIMPLE SUET RECIPE

Ingredients:
2 cups suet or lard
1 cup peanut butter
2 cups yellow cornmeal
2 cups cracked corn
1 cup black oil sunflower seeds

Directions: In a large pot, melt the suet or lard over low heat. Add the peanut butter, stirring until melted and well mixed. Add remaining ingredients, and mix.

Pour into baking pans or forms and allow to cool. Cut into chunks or shapes. Store in freezer.

Birding Citizen Science

RARE BIRD SIGHTINGS

To report unusual bird sightings or possibly hear recordings of where birds have been seen, you can often call prerecorded hotlines detailing such information. Since these hotlines are usually staffed by volunteers, and phone numbers and even the organizations that host them often change, the phone numbers are not listed here. To obtain the numbers or websites, go to your favorite internet search engine, type in something like "rare bird alert hotline New York" and follow the links provided.

BIRD COUNTS AND CITIZEN SCIENCE

Bird watching isn't just a fun pastime; your observations can actually help science. With habitat fragmentation and climate change harming bird populations, it's essential for biologists to have accurate, up-to-date population totals for birds, especially those that are potentially threatened or endangered.

But tracking birds is tricky; that's where two long-running bird-tracking programs—and you—come in. Think of each as a census for the birds. One is **The Christmas Bird Count,** which has been around for 120 years. Held from mid-December to early January, volunteers spread out to count birds in specific areas around each state and the country, with counts occurring in a local area for only one day. (So if you want to join in on the fun, prepare ahead of time!)

Black-capped Chickadee

The **Great Backyard Bird Count** is similar, but it takes place everywhere, and you can participate if you bird for as little as 15 minutes, making it easy to join. It takes place in February.

Frequently Asked Questions

Why aren't birds showing up to my feeders? It's exciting to put up your bird feeders, but you can't always expect birds to show up right away. It takes time for birds to find feeders, so patience is key. Do your best to feed consistently, offer a variety of foods and offer a water source.

What do I do if there's a bird I can't recognize or find in this book? In any given Northeast state, birders have sighted hundreds of different species of birds. This book focuses on common backyard birds; for that reason, most shorebirds, raptors and the like are not included. Once you bird beyond the backyard, check out a field guide to your state. See page 174.

House Finch male

Should I put out a birdbath? What about mosquitoes? Yes! Putting out a birdbath is a great way to attract birds; to prevent mosquito larvae from taking up residence there, purchase a "water wiggler." These devices agitate the water, preventing it from being suitable for mosquitoes. (Plus, the sound of the moving water attracts birds on its own.)

Help! There are squirrels at my feeders. This is an age-old problem. There are a number of possible solutions, from squirrel baffles and greased bird feeder poles, to buying birdseed treated with hot peppers, which squirrels don't like. On the other hand, there are also feeders specifically for squirrels, including more than a few that are quite inventive.

I found an egg/nest/feather. Can I keep it? Disturbing birds, their nests and even keeping their feathers is against the law in nearly all cases. The reason is simple: Many bird species almost went extinct due to unchecked hunting, egg collection and the use of feathers for high-end fashion. Today, migratory birds are protected by federal law. Instead, take some photos of your find and use the internet to attempt to identify it.

I found a baby bird, or an adult bird that is injured. What should I do? If you find a baby bird, chances are its parent is nearby; in most cases, you simply need to leave it be. If you see an injured bird, you can contact your local wildlife rehabilitation facility and follow their instructions/advice.

Rose-breasted Grosbeak

How to Use This Guide

To help you quickly and easily identify birds, this field guide is organized by color. It also only features birds that are commonly seen in average backyards or at bird feeders.

Refer to the color key on the first page, note the color of the bird and then turn to that section. For example, the male Rose-breasted Grosbeak is black-and-white with a red patch on his chest. Because the bird is mostly black-and-white, it will be found in the black-and-white section.

Each color section is also arranged by size, generally with the smaller birds first. Descriptions may indicate the average size as a range, which in some cases reflects size differences between male and female birds. Flip through the pages in the color section to find the bird. If you already know the name of the bird, check the checklist/index for the page number.

*Look for field marks
called out to make
identification easier*

male

female
pg. 85

Common Name
Scientific name

Size: measurement is from head to tip of tail; may include the wingspan

Male: brief description of the male bird; may include breeding, winter or other plumages

Female: brief description of the female bird, which is sometimes different from the male

Juvenile: brief description of the juvenile bird, which often looks like the adult female

Nest: kind of nest the bird builds to raise its young; who builds it; number of broods per year

Eggs: number of eggs you might expect to see in a nest; color and marking

When Seen: the approximate season(s) when you're likely to see the bird; some birds are seen year-round

Food: what the bird eats most of the time (e.g., seeds, insects, fruit, nectar, small mammals, fish); if it typically comes to a bird feeding station

Compare: notes about other birds that look similar and the pages on which they can be found; may include extra information to aid identification

Stan's Notes: Interesting gee-whiz natural history information. This could be something to look or listen for, or something to help positively identify the bird. Also includes remarkable features.

Look for the black head

female
pg. 105

Eastern Towhee

Pipilo erythrophthalmus

Size: 7–8" (18–20 cm)

Male: Mostly black with rusty-brown sides and a white belly. Long black tail with a white tip. Short, stout, pointed bill and rich, red eyes. White wing patches flash in flight.

Female: similar to male but brown instead of black

Juvenile: light brown, a heavily streaked head, chest and belly, long dark tail with white tip

Nest: cup; female builds; 2 broods per year

Eggs: 3–4; creamy white with brown markings

When Seen: spring through fall

Food: insects, seeds, fruit; visits ground feeders

Compare: American Robin (pg. 141) is slightly larger. The Gray Catbird (pg. 139) lacks a black "hood" and rusty sides. Common Grackle (pg. 47) lacks a white belly and has a long thin bill. Male Rose-breasted Grosbeak (pg. 53) has a rosy patch in center of chest.

Stan's Notes: Named for its distinctive "tow-hee" call (given by both sexes) but known mostly for its other characteristic call, which sounds like "drink-your-tea!" Will hop backward with both feet (bilateral scratching), raking up leaf litter to locate insects and seeds. The female broods, but male does the most feeding of young. In southern coastal states, some have red eyes; others have white eyes.

Look for the brown head

male

female
pg. 101

Brown-headed Cowbird

Molothrus ater

Size: 7½" (19 cm)

Male: A glossy black bird with a chocolate-brown head and pointed, sharp gray bill. Dark eyes.

Female: dull brown with a pointed gray bill

Juvenile: similar to female, but dull gray plumage with a streaked chest

Nest: no nest; lays eggs in the nests of other birds

Eggs: 5–7; white with brown markings

When Seen: year-round in southern half of the region; spring through summer in northern half

Food: insects, seeds; will come to seed feeders

Compare: Male Red-winged Blackbird (pg. 45) is slightly larger and has red-and-yellow patches on its upper wings. The Common Grackle (pg. 47) has a long tail and lacks the brown head. European Starling (pg. 43) has a shorter tail.

Stan's Notes: Cowbirds are members of the blackbird family. Known as brood parasites, Brown-headed Cowbirds are the only parasitic birds in the Northeast. Brood parasites lay their eggs in the nests of other birds, leaving the host birds to raise their young. Cowbirds are known to have laid their eggs in the nests of over 200 species of birds. While some birds reject cowbird eggs, most incubate them and raise the young, even to the exclusion of their own. Look for other birds feeding young birds twice their own size. Named "Cowbird" for its habit of following bison and cattle herds to feed on insects flushed up by the animals.

Look for the iridescent feathers

breeding

winter

European Starling
Sturnus vulgaris

Size: 7½" (19 cm)

Male: Glittering, iridescent purplish-black in spring and sum-mer, duller and speckled with white in fall and winter. Long, pointed yellow bill in spring, gray in fall. Pointed wings. Short tail.

Female: same as male

Juvenile: similar to adult, with grayish-brown plumage and a streaked chest

Nest: cavity; male and female line cavity; 2 broods per year

Eggs: 4–6; bluish with brown markings

When Seen: year-round

Food: insects, seeds, fruit; visits seed or suet feeders

Compare: The Common Grackle (pg. 47) has a long tail. Male Brown-headed Cowbird (pg. 41) has a brown head. Look for the shiny dark feathers to help identify the European Starling.

Stan's Notes: One of our most numerous songbirds. Mimics the songs of up to 20 bird species and imitates sounds, including the human voice. Jaws are more powerful when opening rather than closing, enabling the bird to pry open crevices to find insects. Often displaces woodpeckers, chickadees and other cavity-nesting birds. Large families gather with blackbirds in the fall. Not a native bird; 100 starlings were introduced to New York City in 1890–91 from Europe. Bill changes color with the seasons in spring and fall.

*Look for the
red-and-yellow
shoulder patches*

male

female
pg. 111

Red-winged Blackbird

Agelaius phoeniceus

Size: 8½" (21.5 cm)

Male: Jet-black with red-and-yellow patches on the upper wings (epaulets). Pointed black bill.

Female: heavily streaked brown bird with a pointed brown bill and white eyebrows

Juvenile: same as female

Nest: cup; female builds; 2–3 broods per year

Eggs: 3–4; bluish-green with brown markings

When Seen: spring through fall

Food: seeds, insects; visits seed and suet feeders

Compare: The male Brown-headed Cowbird (pg. 41) is smaller, glossier and has a brown head. The bold red-and-yellow epaulets distinguish the male Red-winged from all other blackbirds.

Stan's Notes: One of the most widespread and numerous birds in the Northeast. Found around marshes, wetlands, lakes and rivers. It is a sure sign of spring when these birds return home. Flocks with as many as 10,000 birds have been reported. Males arrive before the females and sing to defend their territory. The male repeats his call from the top of a cattail while showing off his red-and-yellow shoulder patches. The female chooses a mate and often builds her nest over shallow water in a thick stand of cattails. The male can be aggressive when defending the nest. Feeds mostly on seeds in spring and fall, and insects throughout the summer.

Look for the shiny bluish-black head

Common Grackle

Quiscalus quiscula

Size: 11–13" (28–33 cm)

Male: Large iridescent blackbird with a bluish-black head, purplish-brown body, long black tail, a long, thin bill and bright golden eyes.

Female: similar to male, only smaller and duller

Juvenile: similar to female

Nest: cup; female builds; 2 broods per year

Eggs: 4–5; greenish-white with brown markings

When Seen: spring through summer

Food: fruit, seeds, insects; will come to seed and suet feeders

Compare: European Starling (pg. 43) is much smaller with a speckled appearance and a yellow bill during the breeding season. Male Red-winged Blackbird (pg. 45) has bright red-and-yellow shoulder patches (epaulets).

Stan's Notes: Usually nests in small colonies of up to 75 pairs but travels with other blackbird species in large flocks. Known to feed in farm fields. The common name is derived from the Latin word *gracula*, meaning "to croak," for its loud, raspy call. The male holds his tail in a deep V shape during flight. The flight pattern is usually level, as opposed to an undulating movement. Unlike most birds, it has larger muscles for opening its mouth than for closing it, enabling it to pry crevices apart to find hidden insects.

Look for the glossy black feathers

in flight

American Crow

Corvus brachyrhynchos

Size: 18" (45 cm)

Male: All-black bird with a black bill, legs and feet. Can have a purple sheen in direct sunlight.

Female: same as male

Juvenile: same as adult

Nest: platform; female builds; 1 brood per year

Eggs: 4–6; bluish-to-olive with brown markings

When Seen: year-round

Food: fruit, insects, mammals, fish, carrion; comes to seed and suet feeders

Compare: The crow is a familiar bird to almost everyone.

Stan's Notes: A familiar bird, found in all habitats. Imitates other birds and human voices. One of the smartest of all birds and very social, often entertaining itself by provoking chases with other birds. Eats roadkill but rarely hit by vehicles. Can live up to 20 years. Often reuses its nest every year if not taken over by a Great Horned Owl. Unmated birds, known as helpers, help to raise the young. Extended families roost together at night, dispersing daily to hunt. Cannot soar on thermals. Flaps constantly and glides downward. Gathers in huge communal flocks of up to 10,000 birds in winter.

Look for the small, short bill

male

female

Downy Woodpecker

Dryobates pubescens

Size: 6" (15 cm)

Male: A small woodpecker with a white belly and black-and-white spotted wings. Red mark on the back of head and a white stripe down the back. Short black bill.

Female: same as male, but lacks a red mark on head

Juvenile: same as female, some have a red mark near the forehead

Nest: cavity with a round entrance hole; male and female excavate; 1 brood per year

Eggs: 3–5; white without markings

When Seen: year-round

Food: insects, seeds; visits suet and seed feeders

Compare: Hairy Woodpecker (pg. 55) is larger. Look for the shorter, thinner bill to identify the Downy.

Stan's Notes: Abundant and widespread where trees are present. This is perhaps the most common woodpecker in the U.S. Stiff tail feathers help to brace it like a tripod as it clings to a tree. Like other woodpeckers, it has a long, barbed tongue to pull insects from tiny places. Mates drum on branches or hollow logs to announce territory, which is rarely larger than 5 acres (2 ha). Repeats a high-pitched "peek-peek" call. Nest cavity is wider at the bottom than at the top and is lined with fallen woodchips. Male performs most of the brooding. During winter, it will roost in a cavity. Undulates in flight.

*Look for the
rosy-red
breast patch*

male

female
pg. 107

Rose-breasted Grosbeak

Pheucticus ludovicianus

Size: 7–8" (18–20 cm)

Male: A plump black-and-white bird with a large, triangular rose patch in the center of breast. Wing linings are rosy red. Large ivory bill.

Female: heavily streaked bird with obvious white eyebrows and orange-to-yellow wing linings

Juvenile: similar to female

Nest: cup; female and male construct; 1–2 broods per year

Eggs: 3–5; blue-green with brown markings

When Seen: spring through summer

Food: insects, seeds, fruit; comes to seed feeders

Compare: Male is very distinctive with no look-alikes. Look for the rose breast patch to identify.

Stan's Notes: Seen in small groups. Prefers a mature deciduous forest for nesting. Both sexes sing, but the male sings much louder and clearer. Sings a rich, robin-like song with a chip note in the tune. "Grosbeak" refers to the thick, strong bill, which is used to crush seeds. The rose patch varies in size and shape in each male. Males have white wing patches that flash during flight. Males arrive at the breeding grounds a few days before the females. Several males will come to seed feeders together in spring. When the females arrive, males become territorial and reduce their feeder visits. After fledging, young grosbeaks visit feeders with the adults. Makes short flights from tree to tree with rapid wingbeats.

Look for the large bill

male

female

Hairy Woodpecker

Dryobates villosus

Size: 9" (23 cm)

Male: A black-and-white woodpecker with a white belly. Black wings with rows of white spots. White stripe down the back. Long black bill. Red mark on the back of head.

Female: same as male, but lacks a red mark on head

Juvenile: grayer version of the female

Nest: cavity with an oval entrance hole; female and male excavate; 1 brood per year

Eggs: 3–6; white without markings

When Seen: year-round

Food: insects, nuts and seeds; will come to suet and seed feeders

Compare: Much larger than Downy Woodpecker (pg. 51) and has a much longer bill, nearly equal to the width of its head.

Stan's Notes: A common bird in wooded backyards. Announces its arrival with a sharp chirp before landing on feeders. Responsible for eating many destructive forest insects. Uses its barbed tongue to extract insects from trees. Tiny bristle-like feathers at the base of the bill protect the nostrils from wood dust. Drums on hollow logs, branches or stovepipes in spring to announce territory. Often prefers to excavate nest cavities in live aspen trees. Excavates a larger, more oval-shaped entrance than the round entrance hole of the Downy Woodpecker. Makes short flights from tree to tree.

male

*Look for the
black-and-white
striped back*

female

Red-bellied Woodpecker
Melanerpes carolinus

Size: 9–9½" (23–24 cm)

Male: Black-and-white "zebra-backed" woodpecker with a white rump. Red crown extends down the nape of neck. Tan chest. Pale red tinge on the belly, often hard to see.

Female: same as male, but has a light gray crown and a red nape

Juvenile: gray version of adults; lacks a red crown and red nape

Nest: cavity; female and male excavate; 1 brood per year

Eggs: 4–5; white without markings

When Seen: year-round

Food: insects, nuts, fruit; visits suet and seed feeders

Compare: Similar to the Northern Flicker (pg. 117). Look for the zebra-striped back to help identify the Red-bellied Woodpecker.

Stan's Notes: Likes shady woodlands, forest edges and backyards. Digs holes in rotten wood to find spiders, centipedes, beetles and more. Hammers acorns and berries into crevices of trees for winter food. Returns to the same tree to excavate a new nest below that of the previous year. Undulating flight with rapid wingbeats. Gives a loud "querrr" call and a low "chug-chug-chug." Named for the pale-red tinge on its belly. Expanding its range all over the country.

Look for the bright red crest

male

female

Pileated Woodpecker

Dryocopus pileatus

Size: 19" (48 cm)

Male: A crow-sized woodpecker with a black back and bright red forehead, crest and mustache. Long gray bill. White leading edge of wings flash brightly during flight.

Female: same as male, but has a black forehead; lacks a red mustache

Juvenile: similar to adults, only duller and browner

Nest: cavity; male and female excavate; 1 brood per year

Eggs: 3–5; white without markings

When Seen: year-round

Food: insects; will come to suet and peanut feeders

Compare: Unlikely to be confused with any other woodpeckers. Look for the bright red crest and exceptionally large size to identify the Pileated Woodpecker.

Stan's Notes: Our largest woodpecker. The common name comes from the Latin *pileatus*, which means "wearing a cap," referring to its crest. A relatively shy bird that prefers large tracts of woodland. Drums on hollow branches, chimneys and so forth to announce its territory. Excavates oval holes up to several feet long in tree trunks, looking for insects to eat. Large wood chips lie on the ground by excavated trees. Favorite food is carpenter ants. Feeds regurgitated insects to its young. Young emerge from the nest looking just like the adults.

Look for the vibrant blue feathers

male

female
pg. 85

Indigo Bunting
Passerina cyanea

Size: 5½" (14 cm)

Male: Vibrant blue finch-like bird. Dark markings scattered on wings and tail.

Female: light brown bird with faint markings

Juvenile: similar to female

Nest: cup; female builds; 2 broods per year

Eggs: 3–4; pale blue without markings

When Seen: spring through summer

Food: insects, seeds, fruit; will visit seed feeders

Compare: Male Eastern Bluebird (pg. 67) is larger and has a rust-red chest. Look for the bright blue plumage to identify the male Indigo Bunting.

Stan's Notes: Seen along woodland edges and in parks and yards, feeding on insects. Comes to seed feeders early in spring, before insects are plentiful. Usually only the males are noticed. Male often sings from treetops to attract a mate. Female is quiet. Actually a gray bird, without blue pigment in its feathers. Like Blue Jays and other blue birds, sunlight is refracted within the structure of the male's feathers, making them appear blue. Plumage is iridescent in direct sun, duller in shade. Molts in spring to acquire body feathers with gray tips, which quickly wear off, revealing the bright blue plumage. Molts in fall and appears like the female during winter. Migrates at night in flocks of 5–10 birds. Males return before the females and juveniles, often to the nest site of the preceding year. Juveniles move to within a mile of their birth site.

Look for the white chin and chest

Tree Swallow

Tachycineta bicolor

Size: 5–6" (13–15 cm)

Male: Blue-green in spring, greener in fall. Changes color in direct sunlight. White from chin to belly. Long, pointed wing tips. Notched tail.

Female: similar to male, only duller

Juvenile: gray-brown with a white belly and a grayish breast band

Nest: cavity; female and male line a vacant woodpecker cavity or nest box; 2 broods per year

Eggs: 4–6; white without markings

When Seen: spring through fall

Food: insects

Compare: The Barn Swallow (pg. 65) has a rusty belly and a long, deeply forked tail. Look for the white chin, chest and belly and the notched tail to identify the Tree Swallow.

Stan's Notes: Found at ponds, lakes, rivers and farm fields. Often seen flying back and forth across fields, feeding on insects. Can be attracted to your yard with a nest box. Competes with the Eastern Bluebird for tree cavities and nest boxes. Builds a grass nest within and will travel long distances, looking for dropped feathers for the lining. Watch for it playing, chasing after feathers. Flies with rapid wingbeats, then glides. Gives a series of gurgles and chirps. Chatters when upset or threatened. Eats many nuisance bugs, so it's good to have around. Families gather in large flocks for migration.

*Look for the
deeply forked tail*

Barn Swallow
Hirundo rustica

Size: 7" (18 cm)

Male: A sleek swallow. Blue-black back, cinnamon belly and reddish-brown chin. White spots on a long, deeply forked tail.

Female: same as male, but has a whitish belly

Juvenile: similar to adults, with a tan belly and chin and a shorter tail

Nest: cup; female and male build; 2 broods per year

Eggs: 4–5; white with brown markings

When Seen: spring through fall

Food: insects (prefers beetles, wasps, flies)

Compare: Tree Swallow (pg. 63) is white from chin to belly. Look for the deeply forked tail to help identify the Barn Swallow.

Stan's Notes: Seen in wetlands, farms, suburban yards and parks. The Northeast has six swallow species, but this is the only one with a deeply forked tail. Unlike other swallows, it rarely glides in flight. Usually flies low over land or water. Drinks as it flies, skimming water, or will sip water droplets on wet leaves. Bathes while flying through rain or sprinklers. Gives a twittering warble, followed by a mechanical sound. Builds a mud nest with up to 1,000 beak-loads of mud. Nests on barns, houses, under bridges and other sheltered places. Often nests in colonies of 4–6 birds; sometimes nests alone.

male

Look for the
rusty-red chest

Look for the
gray head and
blue back

female

Eastern Bluebird

Sialia sialis

Size: 7" (18 cm)

Male: Sky-blue head, back and tail. Rust-red breast and white belly.

Female: grayer than the male, with a faint rusty breast and faint blue wings and tail

Juvenile: similar to female, but spots on the breast and blue wing markings

Nest: cavity, vacant woodpecker cavity or nest box; female adds a soft lining; 2 broods per year

Eggs: 4–5; pale blue without markings

When Seen: from spring through early winter

Food: insects, fruit; comes to shallow dishes with live or dead mealworms, and to suet feeders

Compare: The male Indigo Bunting (pg. 61) is nearly all blue. The Blue Jay (pg. 69) is much larger and has a crest. Look for the rusty breast to help identify the Eastern Bluebird.

Stan's Notes: Nearly eliminated due to a lack of nest cavities. Thanks to people who installed thousands of nest boxes, bluebirds now thrive. Prefers open habitats, such as farm fields, pastures and roadsides, but also likes forest edges, parks and yards. Easily tamed. Often perches on trees or fence posts and drops to the ground to grab bugs, especially grasshoppers. Makes short flights from tree to tree. Song is a distinctive "churlee chur chur-lee." The rust-red breast is like that of the American Robin (pg. 141), its cousin. The young of the first brood help raise the second brood.

Look for the large crest

Blue Jay
Cyanocitta cristata

Size: 12" (30 cm)

Male: Bright light-blue-and-white bird with a black necklace and gray belly. Large crest moves up and down at will. White face, wing bars and tip of tail. Black tail bands.

Female: same as male

Juvenile: same as adult, only duller

Nest: cup; female and male construct; 1–2 broods per year

Eggs: 4–5; green to blue with brown markings

When Seen: year-round

Food: insects, fruit, carrion, seeds, nuts; visits seed feeders, ground feeders with corn or peanuts

Compare: The Eastern Bluebird (pg. 67) is much smaller and has a rust-red breast. Look for the large crest to help identify the Blue Jay.

Stan's Notes: A highly intelligent bird, solving problems, gathering food and communicating more than other birds. Loud, noisy and mimics other birds. Known as the alarm of the forest, screaming at intruders. Imitates hawk calls around feeders to scare off other birds. One of the few birds to cache food. Can remember where it hid thousands of nuts. Carries seeds and nuts in a pouch under its tongue (sublingual). Eats bird eggs and young birds in other nests. Feathers lack blue pigment; refracted sunlight casts the blue light.

Look for the thin, curved bill

Brown Creeper
Certhia americana

Size: 5" (13 cm)

Male: Small, thin, nearly camouflaged brown bird. White from chin to belly. White eyebrows. Dark eyes and a thin, curved bill. Tail is long and stiff.

Female: same as male

Juvenile: same as adult

Nest: cup; female constructs; 1 brood per year

Eggs: 5–6; white with tiny brown markings

When Seen: year-round

Food: insects, nuts, seeds

Compare: Red-breasted Nuthatch (pg. 127) and White-breasted Nuthatch (pg. 131) climb down tree trunks, not up. To spot a Brown Creeper, look for a small brown bird with a white belly creeping up trees.

Stan's Notes: A forest bird, commonly found in wooded habitats. Will fly from the top of one tree trunk to the bottom of another, then work its way to the top, looking for caterpillars, spider eggs and more. Its long tail has tiny spines underneath, which help it cling to trees. Uses its camouflage coloring to hide in plain sight. Spreads out flat on a branch or trunk and won't move. Often builds its nest behind the loose bark of a dead or dying tree. Young follow their parents around, creeping up trees soon after fledging.

Look for the rusty crown

Chipping Sparrow

Spizella passerina

Size: 5" (13 cm)

Male: Small gray-brown sparrow with a clear gray chest, white eyebrows, thin black eye line and rusty crown. Thin gray-black bill. Two faint wing bars.

Female: same as male

Juvenile: similar to adult, with streaking on the chest; lacks a rusty crown

Nest: cup; female builds; 2 broods per year

Eggs: 3–5; blue-green with brown markings

When Seen: spring through summer

Food: insects, seeds; will come to ground feeders

Compare: American Tree Sparrow (pg. 89) has gray eyebrows and a rusty eye line. The Fox Sparrow (pg. 99) and female House Finch (pg. 79) have heavily streaked chests. Look for the rusty crown and black eye line to identify the Chipping Sparrow.

Stan's Notes: A common garden or yard bird, often seen feeding on dropped seeds beneath feeders. Gathers in large family groups to feed in preparation for migration. Migrates at night in flocks of 20–30 birds. The common name comes from the male's fast "chip" call. Often just called Chippy. Builds nest low in dense shrubs and almost always lines it with animal hair. Comfortable with people, allowing you to approach closely before it flies away.

Look for the bright red crown

male

female

Common Redpoll
Acanthis flammea

Size: 5" (13 cm)

Male: A sparrow-like bird with a bright red crown and raspberry-red on the chest. Black spot on the chin. Heavily streaked back.

Female: similar to male, but lacks raspberry-red on the chest

Juvenile: browner than adults, with dark streaking on the chest; lacks a red crown

Nest: cup; female builds; 1 brood (occasionally 2) per year

Eggs: 4–5; pale green with purple markings

When Seen: fall and winter

Food: seeds, insects; will come to seed feeders

Compare: Pine Siskin (pg. 77) has yellow wing bars and a streaked chest. Look for the bright red crown and black spot under the bill to help identify the Common Redpoll.

Stan's Notes: Moves from location to location, wheeling around in the sky before landing at feeders. Visits feeders in small to large flocks. Flocks of up 100 birds are not uncommon but not seen at all in some winters. Bathes in open water or snow during winter. Like the Black-capped Chickadee, it can be tamed and hand fed. Gives a zipping call in long strings that last 30 seconds or more. Also gives a nasal, rising whistle.

Look for the
yellow on the wings

Pine Siskin

Spinus pinus

Size: 5" (13 cm)

Male: Small brown finch with heavy streaking on the back, breast and belly. Yellow wing bars. Yellow at the base of tail. Thin bill.

Female: similar to male, with less yellow

Juvenile: similar to adult, with a light yellow tinge over the breast and chin

Nest: cup; female builds; 2 broods

Eggs: 3–4; greenish-blue with brown markings

When Seen: fall and winter

Food: seeds, insects; will come to seed feeders

Compare: Female Purple Finch (pg. 93) has white eyebrows. Female House Finch (pg. 79) lacks any yellow. Female American Goldfinch (pg. 163) has white wing bars. Look for the yellow wing bars to identify the Pine Siskin.

Stan's Notes: Usually considered a winter finch. Conspicuous in some winters, rare in others. Seen in flocks of up to 20 birds, often with other finch species. Gathers in flocks and moves around, visiting feeders. Will come to thistle feeders. Gives a series of high-pitched, wheezy calls. Also gives a wheezing twitter. Breeds in small groups. Builds nest toward the end of coniferous branches, where needles are dense, helping to conceal. Nests are often only a few feet apart. Male feeds the female during incubation. Juveniles lose the yellow tint by late summer of their first year.

male
pg. 157

female

Look for the
heavily streaked chest

House Finch

Haemorhous mexicanus

Size: 5" (13 cm)

Female: Plain brown bird with heavy streaking on a white chest.

Male: red-to-orange face, throat, chest and rump, brown cap, brown marking behind the eyes, streaked belly and wings

Juvenile: similar to female

Nest: cup, occasionally in a cavity, female builds; 2 broods per year

Eggs: 4–5; pale blue, lightly marked

When Seen: year-round

Food: seeds, fruit, leaf buds; visits seed feeders and feeders that offer grape jelly

Compare: The female Purple Finch (pg. 93) has bold white eyebrows. Pine Siskin (pg. 77) has yellow wing bars and a smaller bill. Female American Goldfinch (pg. 163) has a clear chest. Look for the heavily streaked chest to help identify the female House Finch.

Stan's Notes: Can be a common bird at your feeders. A very social bird, visiting feeders in small flocks. Likes to nest in hanging flower baskets. Male sings a loud, cheerful warbling song. It was originally introduced to Long Island, New York, from the western U.S. in the 1940s. Now found throughout the country. Suffers from a disease that causes the eyes to crust, resulting in blindness and death.

Look for the slightly curved bill

House Wren

Troglodytes aedon

Size: 5" (13 cm)

Male: All-brown bird with lighter brown markings on the wings and tail. Slightly curved brown bill. Often holds tail upward.

Female: same as male

Juvenile: same as adult

Nest: cavity; female and male line just about any nest cavity; 2 broods per year

Eggs: 4–6; tan with brown markings

When Seen: spring to fall

Food: insects, spiders, snails

Compare: Carolina Wren (pg. 83) has prominent eyebrows. The slightly curved bill and upward position of the tail differentiate the House Wren from sparrows. All other species of wrens have eyebrows. Look for the curved bill and upturned tail to help identify the House Wren.

Stan's Notes: A prolific songster. During the mating season, sings from dawn to dusk. Seen in brushy yards, parks, woodlands and along forest edges. Easily attracted to a nest box. In spring, the male chooses several prospective nesting cavities and places a few small twigs in each. The female inspects all of them and finishes constructing the nest in the cavity of her choice. She fills the cavity with short twigs and then lines a small depression at the back with pine needles and grass. She often has trouble fitting longer twigs through the entrance hole and tries many different directions and approaches until she is successful.

*Look for the
bold white eyebrows*

Carolina Wren

Thryothorus ludovicianus

Size: 5½" (14 cm)

Male: Rusty-brown head and back with an orange-yellow chest and belly. White throat and a prominent white eye stripe. Short, stubby tail, often cocked up.

Female: same as male

Juvenile: same as adults

Nest: cavity; female and male build; 2 broods per year, sometimes 3

Eggs: 4–6; white, sometimes pink or creamy, with brown markings

When Seen: year-round

Food: insects, fruit, few seeds; visits suet feeders

Compare: House Wren (pg. 81) is darker brown and lacks a white eye stripe.

Stan's Notes: Mates are long-term, staying together throughout the year in permanent territories. Sings year-round. The male is known to sing up to 40 song types, singing one song repeatedly before switching to another. The female also sings, resulting in duets. The male often takes over feeding the first brood while the female renests. Nests in birdhouses and in unusual places like mailboxes, bumpers or broken taillights of vehicles, or nearly any other cavity. Found in brushy yards or woodlands. Can be attracted to feeders with mealworms.

male
pg. 61

female

Look for the
faint blue
on the wings

Indigo Bunting
Passerina cyanea

Size: 5½" (14 cm)

Female: A light brown finch-like bird. Faint streaking on a light tan chest. Wings have a very faint blue cast and indistinct wing bars.

Male: vibrant blue with scattered dark markings on wings and tail

Juvenile: similar to female

Nest: cup; female builds; 2 broods per year

Eggs: 3–4; pale blue without markings

When Seen: spring to summer

Food: insects, seeds, fruit; will visit seed feeders

Compare: Female Purple Finch (pg. 93) has white eyebrows and heavy streaking on the chest. Female House Finch (pg. 79) has a heavily streaked chest. Female American Goldfinch (pg. 163) has white wing bars. Look for the faint blue cast on the wings to help identify the female Indigo Bunting.

Stan's Notes: Seen along woodland edges and in parks and yards, feeding on insects. Comes to seed feeders early in spring, before insects are plentiful. Secretive, plain and quiet, usually only the males are noticed. Male often sings from treetops to attract a mate. Migrates at night in flocks of 5–10 birds. Males return before the females and juveniles, often to the nest site of the preceding year. Juveniles move to within a mile of their birth site.

Look for the ivory-to-pink bill

male
pg. 133

female

Dark-eyed Junco
Junco hyemalis

Size: 5½" (14 cm)

Female: A plump, dark-eyed bird with a tan-to-brown chest, head and back. White belly. Ivory-to-pink bill. White outer tail feathers appear like a white V in flight.

Male: round bird with gray plumage

Juvenile: similar to female, with streaking on the breast and head

Nest: cup; female and male build; 2 broods per year

Eggs: 3–5; white with reddish-brown markings

When Seen: fall to winter; year-round in some areas

Food: seeds, insects; visits ground and seed feeders

Compare: Rarely confused with any other bird. Look for the ivory-to-pink bill and small flocks feeding under feeders to help identify the female Dark-eyed Junco.

Stan's Notes: One of the most common winter birds in the Northeast. Migrates from Canada and northern parts of Minnesota to areas farther south. Adheres to a rigid social hierarchy, with dominant birds chasing the less dominant birds. Look for the white outer tail feathers flashing in flight. Often seen in small flocks on the ground, where it uses its feet to simultaneously "double-scratch" to expose seeds and insects. Eats many weed seeds. Nests in a wide variety of wooded habitats. Several subspecies of Dark-eyed Junco were previously considered to be separate species.

Look for the rusty crown and eye line

American Tree Sparrow

Spizelloides arborea

Size: 6" (15 cm)

Male: Brown bird with a tan chest and rusty crown and eye line. Gray eyebrows. Dark spot in the center of chest. Dark upper bill, yellow lower bill. Two white wing bars.

Female: same as male

Juvenile: streaked chest often obscures the central dark spot; lacks a rusty crown

Nest: cup; female builds; 1 brood per year

Eggs: 3–5; greenish-white with brown markings

When Seen: fall and winter

Food: insects, seeds; visits seed feeders

Compare: Chipping Sparrow (pg. 73) has white eyebrows and a black eye line. To identify the American Tree Sparrow, check for the dark spot on the chest and the two-toned bill.

Stan's Notes: A regular feeder visitor in some places in the Northeast during winter. Seen during migration in flocks of 2–200 birds. Found in open fields, woodlands and suburban backyards. Sometimes called Winter Chippy because it looks like the Chipping Sparrow. Gives a series of high-pitched, sweet-sounding whistles. Nests in Canada and Alaska. The species name *arborea* means "tree," but it doesn't nest in trees. Nests on the ground in a clump of grass. The name "Tree" refers to its habitat. "American" refers to its natural range.

Look for the black throat patch

male

Look for the tan stripe through the eye

female

House Sparrow
Passer domesticus

Size: 6" (15 cm)

Male: Brown back with a gray belly and cap. Large black patch extending from the throat to the chest (bib). One white wing bar.

Female: slightly smaller than the male, light brown with light eyebrows; lacks a bib and white wing bar

Juvenile: similar to female

Nest: cavity; female and male build a domed cup nest within; 2–3 broods per year

Eggs: 4–6; white with brown markings

When Seen: year-round

Food: seeds, insects, fruit; comes to seed feeders

Compare: The American Tree Sparrow (pg. 89) and the Chipping Sparrow (pg. 73) have a rusty crown. Look for the black bib to identify the male House Sparrow and the clear breast to help identify the female.

Stan's Notes: One of the first birdsongs heard in cities in spring. A familiar city bird, nearly always in small flocks. Also found on farms. Introduced from Europe in 1850 to Central Park in New York. Now seen throughout North America. Related to Old World sparrows; not a relative of any sparrows in the U.S. An aggressive bird that will kill young birds in order to take over the nest cavity. Uses dried grass, small scraps of plastic, paper and other materials to build an oversized domed nest in the cavity.

*Look for
the bold
white eyebrows*

male
pg. 159

female

Purple Finch

Haemorhous purpureus

Size:	6" (15 cm)
Female:	Plain brown bird with heavy streaking on the chest, bold white eyebrows and a large bill.
Male:	raspberry-red head, cap, breast, back and rump, brownish wings and tail
Juvenile:	same as female
Nest:	cup; female and male build; 1 brood per year
Eggs:	4–5; greenish-blue with brown markings
When Seen:	year-round
Food:	seeds, insects, fruit; comes to seed feeders
Compare:	Female House Finch (pg. 79) lacks eyebrows. Pine Siskin (pg. 77) has yellow wing bars. Female American Goldfinch (pg. 163) has a clear chest. Look for the bold white eyebrows to identify the female Purple Finch.

Stan's Notes: An irruptive migrator, seen in the Northeast at different times of the year but not always here every winter. Travels in flocks of up to 50 birds. Visits seed feeders along with House Finches, which makes it hard to tell them apart. Ash tree seeds are an important source of food; feeds mainly on seeds. Found in coniferous forests, mixed woods, woodland edges and suburban backyards. Flies in the typical undulating, up-and-down pattern of finches. Sings a rich, loud song. Gives a distinctive "tic" note only in flight. Male is not purple. The Latin species name *purpureus* means "purple" or other reddish colors.

Look for the light stripes on the head

white-striped

Look for the light stripes on the head

tan-striped

White-throated Sparrow
Zonotrichia albicollis

Size: 6–7" (15–18 cm)

Male: Brown sparrow with a gray or tan chest and belly, and a white or tan throat patch and eyebrows. Bold striping on the head. Small yellow spot by each eye (lore).

Female: same as male

Juvenile: similar to adult, with a heavily streaked chest and gray throat and eyebrows

Nest: cup; female builds; 1 brood per year

Eggs: 4–6; green to blue or cream-white with red-brown markings

When Seen: spring and fall migration

Food: insects, seeds, fruit; visits ground feeders

Compare: White-crowned Sparrow (pg. 97) lacks the throat patch and yellow lores of the White-throated Sparrow.

Stan's Notes: Two color variations (polymorphic): white-striped and tan-striped. Studies indicate that the white-striped adults tend to mate with the tan-striped birds. It's not clear why. Known for its wonderful song. Sings all year and can even be heard at night. White- and tan-striped males and white-striped females sing, but tan-striped females do not. Builds nest on the ground under small trees in bogs and coniferous forests. Often associated with other sparrows in winter. Feeds on the ground under feeders. Immature and first-year females tend to winter farther south than the adults.

Look for the
black-and-white striped crown

juvenile

White-crowned Sparrow

Zonotrichia leucophrys

Size: 6½–7½" (16.5–19 cm)

Male: Brown with a gray chest and black-and-white striped crown. Small, thin pink bill.

Female: same as male

Juvenile: similar to adult, with black-and-brown stripes on the head

Nest: cup; female builds; 2 broods per year

Eggs: 3–5; greenish to bluish to whitish, with red-brown markings

When Seen: spring and fall migration

Food: insects, seeds, berries; visits ground feeders

Compare: The White-throated Sparrow (pg. 95) has a throat patch and a small yellow spot by each eye (lore). Look for the striped crown to help identify the White-crowned Sparrow.

Stan's Notes: Often in groups of up to 20 birds during migration, when it can be seen visiting ground feeders and feeding beneath seed feeders. A ground feeder that will "double-scratch" backward with both feet simultaneously to find seeds. Prefers scrubby areas, woodland edges and open or grassy habitats. The males are prolific songsters, singing in late winter while migrating northward. Males arrive at the breeding grounds before the females and sing from perches to establish territory. Males take most of the responsibility to raise the young while females start a second brood. Only 9–12 days separate the broods.

Look for the heavy streaks on the chest

Fox Sparrow

Passerella iliaca

Size: 7" (18 cm)

Male: A plump, rust-red sparrow. Heavily streaked rusty breast and solid rust tail. Head and back are mottled with gray.

Female: same as male

Juvenile: same as adult

Nest: cup; female builds; 2 broods per year

Eggs: 2–4; pale green with reddish markings

When Seen: spring and fall migration

Food: seeds, insects; comes to ground feeders

Compare: The Brown Thrasher (pg. 115) is much larger, slimmer and has a long, curved bill. The rust-red plumage of the Fox Sparrow differentiates it from all other sparrows.

Stan's Notes: One of the largest sparrows. Often alone or in small groups. Found in shrubby areas, open fields and backyards. Comes to ground feeders and seen underneath seed feeders during migration, searching for seeds and insects. Like a chicken, it will "double-scratch" with both feet at the same time to look for food. Gives a series of rich notes lasting 2–3 seconds, usually singing from a perch hidden in a shrub. The common name "Sparrow" comes from the Anglo-Saxon word *spearwa*, meaning "flutterer," and applies to any small bird. "Fox" refers to its rusty color. Appears in several color variations, depending on the part of the country. Nests on the ground in brush and along forest edges in Canada and Alaska.

*Look for the
pointed gray bill*

female

male
pg. 41

Brown-headed Cowbird

Molothrus ater

Size:	7½" (19 cm)
Female:	Dull brown bird with no obvious markings. Pointed, sharp gray bill. Dark eyes.
Male:	glossy black with a chocolate-brown head
Juvenile:	similar to female, but dull gray plumage with a streaked chest
Nest:	no nest; lays eggs in the nests of other birds
Eggs:	5–7; white with brown markings
When Seen:	year-round in southern half of the region; spring through summer in northern half
Food:	insects, seeds; will come to seed feeders
Compare:	Female Red-winged Blackbird (pg. 111) has white eyebrows and heavy streaking. Female Indigo Bunting (pg. 85) has faint blue on its wings. Look for the pointed gray bill to help identify the female Brown-headed Cowbird.

Stan's Notes: Cowbirds are members of the blackbird family. Known as brood parasites, Brown-headed Cowbirds are the only parasitic birds in the Northeast. Brood parasites lay their eggs in the nests of other birds, leaving the host birds to raise their young. Cowbirds are known to have laid their eggs in the nests of over 200 species of birds. While some birds reject cowbird eggs, most incubate them and raise the young, even to the exclusion of their own. Look for other birds feeding young birds twice their own size. Named "Cowbird" for its habit of following bison and cattle herds to feed on insects flushed up by the animals.

1 year old

Look for the waxy-looking red wing tips

Bohemian Waxwing

Cedar Waxwing

Bombycilla cedrorum

Size: 7½" (19 cm)

Male: A sleek-looking gray-to-brown bird. Pointed crest, bandit-like mask and light yellow belly. Bold yellow tip of tail. Red wing tips look like they were dipped in red wax.

Female: same as male

Juvenile: grayish with a heavily streaked breast; lacks a sleek look, black mask and red wing tips

Nest: cup; female and male construct; 1 brood per year, occasionally 2

Eggs: 4–6; pale blue with brown markings

When Seen: year-round

Food: cedar cones, fruit, seeds, insects

Compare: The female Northern Cardinal (pg. 161) has a large red bill. Bohemian Waxwing (see inset), is larger, less common and has white on its wings and rust under its tail. Look for the red wing tips to help identify the Cedar Waxwing.

Stan's Notes: The name is derived from its red wax-like wing tips and preference for the small, berry-like cones of the cedar. Seen in flocks, moving around from area to area, looking for berries. Feeds on insects during summer, before berries are abundant. Wanders during winter, searching for food supplies. Spends most of its time at the top of tall trees. Listen for the high-pitched "sreee" whistling sound it constantly makes while perched or in flight. Obtains the mask after the first year and red wing tips after the second year.

male
pg. 39

female

Look for the rusty sides

Eastern Towhee

Pipilo erythrophthalmus

Size: 7–8" (18–20 cm)

Female: Mostly light-brown bird. Rusty red-brown sides and a white belly. Long brown tail with a white tip. Short, stout, pointed bill and rich, red eyes. White wing patches flash in flight.

Male: similar to female but black instead of brown

Juvenile: light brown, a heavily streaked head, chest and belly, long dark tail with white tip

Nest: cup; female builds; 2 broods per year

Eggs: 3–4; creamy white with brown markings

When Seen: spring through fall

Food: insects, seeds, fruit; visits ground feeders

Compare: The American Robin (pg. 141) is larger, has a red breast and lacks the white belly. The female Rose-breasted Grosbeak (pg. 107) has a heavily streaked breast and obvious white eyebrows.

Stan's Notes: Named for its distinctive "tow-hee" call, given by both sexes, but known mostly for its other characteristic call, which sounds like "drink-your-tea!" Will hop backward with both feet (double-scratching), raking up leaf litter to locate insects and seeds. The female does the brooding. The male feeds the young most of the time. In southern coastal states, some have red eyes; others have white eyes.

Look for the large white eyebrows

female

male
pg. 53

Rose-breasted Grosbeak

Pheucticus ludovicianus

Size: 7–8" (18–20 cm)

Female: Plump and heavily streaked. Large, obvious white eyebrows. Large ivory bill. Orange-to-yellow wing linings.

Male: black-and-white with a triangular rose patch in the center of chest, rose-red wing linings

Juvenile: similar to female

Nest: cup; female and male construct; 1–2 broods per year

Eggs: 3–5; blue-green with brown markings

When Seen: spring to summer

Food: insects, seeds, fruit; comes to seed feeders

Compare: Looks like a large finch with bold white eyebrows and heavy streaking. Female Purple Finch (pg. 93) has smaller eyebrows. Female House Finch (pg. 79) lacks eyebrows.

Stan's Notes: Seen in small groups. Prefers a mature deciduous forest for nesting. Both sexes sing, but the male sings much louder and clearer. Sings a rich, robin-like song with a chip note in the tune. "Grosbeak" refers to the thick, strong bill, which is used to crush seeds. Males arrive at the breeding grounds a few days before females. Several males will visit seed feeders together in spring. When females arrive, males become territorial and reduce the feeder visits. After fledging, young grosbeaks visit feeders with adults. Makes short flights from tree to tree with rapid wingbeats.

Look for the reddish bill

male
pg. 161

female

juvenile

Northern Cardinal
Cardinalis cardinalis

Size: 8–9" (20–23 cm)

Female: Buff-brown with a black mask, large reddish bill and red tinges on the crest and wings.

Male: red with a large crest and bill, black mask extending from the face to the throat

Juvenile: same as female, but with a blackish-gray bill

Nest: cup; female builds; 2–3 broods per year

Eggs: 3–4; bluish-white with brown markings

When Seen: year-round

Food: seeds, insects, fruit; comes to seed feeders

Compare: The Cedar Waxwing (pg. 103) has a small dark bill. The juvenile Northern Cardinal (see inset) looks like the adult female Cardinal, but the juvenile has a dark bill. Look for the reddish bill to identify the female Northern Cardinal.

Stan's Notes: A familiar backyard bird. Seen in a variety of habitats, including parks. Usually likes thick vegetation. One of the few species in which both females and males sing. Can be heard all year. Listen for its "whata-cheer-cheer-cheer" territorial call in spring. Watch for a male feeding a female during courtship. The male also feeds the young of the first brood while the female builds a second nest. Territorial in spring, fighting its own reflection in a window or other reflective surface. Non-territorial in winter, gathering in small flocks of up to 20 birds. Makes short flights from cover, often landing on the ground. *Cardinalis* denotes importance, as represented by the red garments of Catholic cardinals.

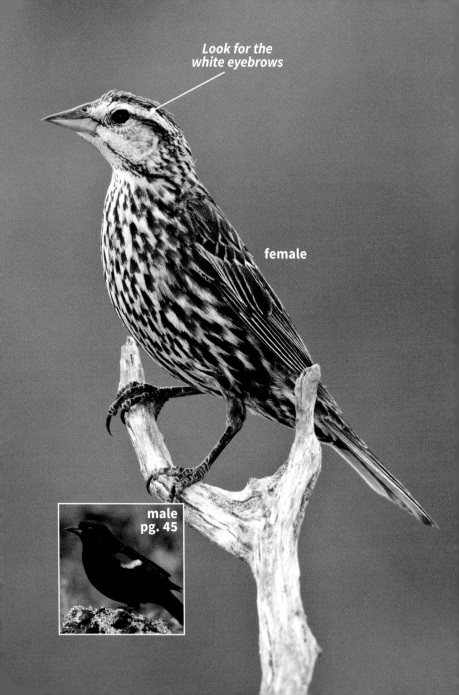

Look for the white eyebrows

female

male
pg. 45

Red-winged Blackbird
Agelaius phoeniceus

Size: 8½" (21.5 cm)

Female: Heavily streaked brown bird with a pointed brown bill and white eyebrows.

Male: jet-black bird with red-and-yellow shoulder patches (epaulets) and a pointed black bill

Juvenile: same as female

Nest: cup; female builds; 2–3 broods per year

Eggs: 3–4; bluish-green with brown markings

When Seen: spring to fall

Food: seeds, insects; visits seed and suet feeders

Compare: Female Rose-breasted Grosbeak (pg. 107) is more plump and has a thicker bill. Female Brown-headed Cowbird (pg. 101) lacks any streaks. Look for white eyebrows and heavy streaking to identify the female Red-winged.

Stan's Notes: One of the most widespread and numerous birds in the Northeast. Found around marshes, wetlands, lakes and rivers. It is a sure sign of spring when these birds return home. Flocks with as many as 10,000 birds have been reported. Males arrive before the females and sing to defend their territory. The male repeats his call from the top of a cattail while showing off his red-and-yellow shoulder patches. The female chooses a mate and often builds her nest over shallow water in a thick stand of cattails. The male can be aggressive when defending the nest. Feeds mostly on seeds in spring and fall, and insects throughout the summer.

Look for the
two black neck bands

Killdeer
Charadrius vociferus

Size: 11" (28 cm)

Male: An upland shorebird with two black bands around the neck, like a necklace. Brown back and white belly. Bright reddish-orange rump, visible in flight.

Female: same as male

Juvenile: similar to adult, with a single neck band

Nest: ground; male scrapes; 2 broods per year

Eggs: 3–5; tan with brown markings

When Seen: spring to fall

Food: insects; also worms, snails

Compare: By virtue of its habitat, there's not a lot you can confuse with the Killdeer.

Stan's Notes: Technically classified as a shorebird but lives in dry habitats instead of the shore. Often found in vacant fields, gravel pits, driveways, wetland edges or along railroad tracks. The only shorebird that has two black neck bands. Known to fake a broken wing to draw intruders away from the nest. Once the nest is safe, the parent will take flight. Nests are just a slight depression in a dry area and are often hard to see. Hatchlings look like miniature adults walking on stilts. Soon after hatching, the young follow their parents around and peck for insects. Gives a loud and distinctive "kill-deer" call. Migrates in small flocks.

Look for the long, rusty-red tail

Brown Thrasher

Toxostoma rufum

Size: 11" (28 cm)

Male: Rust-red with a long tail. Heavy streaking on the breast and belly. Two white wing bars. Long, curved bill and bright yellow eyes.

Female: same as male

Juvenile: same as adult, but eyes are grayish

Nest: cup; female and male build; 2 broods per year

Eggs: 4–5; pale blue with brown markings

When Seen: spring to fall

Food: insects, fruit

Compare: Fox Sparrow (pg. 99) has a similar rust-red coloration, but the Thrasher is much larger, thinner, and has a longer bill and tail. Look for the long rust-red tail to help identify the Brown Thrasher.

Stan's Notes: A prodigious songster. Sings along forest edges and in suburban yards. Often in thick shrubs, where it sings deliberate musical phrases, repeating each twice. The male Brown Thrasher has the largest documented repertoire of all North American songbirds, with more than 1,100 types of songs. Builds nest low in dense shrubs, often in fencerows. Quickly flies or runs on the ground in and out of thick shrubs. A noisy feeder due to its habit of turning over leaves, small rocks and branches to find food.

Look for the black mustache

male

female

Northern Flicker
Colaptes auratus

Size:	12" (30 cm)
Male:	Brown-and-black with a black mustache and black necklace. Red spot on the nape of neck. Speckled chest. Large white rump patch, seen only when flying.
Female:	same as male, but lacks a black mustache
Juvenile:	same as adult of the same sex
Nest:	cavity; female and male excavate; 1 brood per year
Eggs:	5–8; white without markings
When Seen:	spring, summer and fall, a few stay for winter
Food:	insects (especially ants and beetles); comes to suet feeders
Compare:	The male Red-bellied Woodpecker (pg. 57) has a red crown. Flickers are the only brown-backed woodpeckers in the Northeast.

Stan's Notes: This is the only woodpecker to regularly feed on the ground. Prefers ants and beetles and produces an antacid saliva that neutralizes the acidic defense of ants. The male often picks the nest site. Parents take up to 12 days to excavate the cavity. Can be attracted to your yard with a nest box stuffed with sawdust. Often reuses an old nest. Undulates deeply during flight, flashing yellow under its wings and tail, and calling "wacka-wacka" loudly.

Look for the small head

Mourning Dove
Zenaida macroura

Size: 12" (30 cm)

Male: Smooth, fawn-colored dove. Gray patch on the head. Iridescent pink and greenish-blue on neck. Single black spot behind and below eyes. Black spots on wings and tail. Pointed, wedged tail with white edges, seen in flight.

Female: similar to male, but lacks the pink-and-green iridescent neck feathers

Juvenile: spotted and streaked plumage

Nest: platform; female and male build; 2 broods per year

Eggs: 2; white without markings

When Seen: spring through fall with a few that stay all winter

Food: seeds; will visit ground and seed feeders

Compare: Lacks the wide range of color combinations of the Rock Pigeon (pg. 147).

Stan's Notes: Name comes from its mournful cooing. A ground feeder, bobbing its head as it walks. One of the few birds to drink without lifting its head, same as the Rock Pigeon. Parents feed the young (squab) a regurgitated liquid called crop-milk during their first few days of life. Platform nest is so flimsy that it often falls apart in a storm. During takeoff and in flight, wind rushes through its wing feathers, creating a characteristic whistling sound.

Look for the dark eyes

Barred Owl
Strix varia

Size: 20–24" (51–61 cm); up to 3½' wingspan

Male: A chunky brown-and-gray owl with a large head and dark brown eyes. Dark horizontal barring on upper chest. Vertical streaks on lower chest and belly. Yellow bill and feet.

Female: same as male, only slightly larger

Juvenile: light gray with a black face

Nest: cavity; does not add nesting material; 1 brood per year

Eggs: 2–3; white without markings

When Seen: year-round

Food: mice, rabbits and other mammals, small birds, fish, reptiles, amphibians

Compare: Lacks the "horns" of the Great Horned Owl (pg. 123). Look for a stocky owl with a large head and dark brown eyes to identify the Barred Owl.

Stan's Notes: A very common owl in the region. Prefers deciduous, dense woodlands with sparse undergrowth, but it can be attracted to your yard with a simple nest box that has a large entrance hole. Often seen hunting during the day. Perches and watches for mice, birds and other prey. Hovers over water and reaches down to grab a fish. After fledging, the young stay with their parents for up to four months. Often sounds like a dog barking just before calling 6–8 hoots, sounding like "who-who-who-cooks-for-you."

Look for the feather tufts on the head

Great Horned Owl

Bubo virginianus

Size: 21–25" (53–64 cm); up to 4' wingspan

Male: A robust brown "horned" owl. Bright yellow eyes and V-shaped white throat, resembling a necklace. Horizontal barring on the chest.

Female: same as male, only slightly larger

Juvenile: similar to adults, but lacks ear tufts

Nest: no nest; takes over the nest of a crow, hawk or Great Blue Heron, or uses a partial cavity, stump or broken tree; 1 brood per year

Eggs: 2–3; white without markings

When Seen: year-round

Food: mammals, birds (ducks), snakes, insects

Compare: Barred Owl (pg. 121) is stocky and has dark eyes. Look for bright yellow eyes and feather "horns" on the head to help identify the Great Horned Owl.

Stan's Notes: One of the earliest nesting birds in the Northeast, laying eggs in January and February. Can hear a mouse move beneath a leaf pile or a foot of snow. "Ears" are tufts of feathers (horns) and have nothing to do with hearing. Cannot turn its head all the way around. Wing feathers are ragged on the ends, resulting in silent flight. Eyelids close from the top down, like ours. Fearless, it is one of the few animals that will kill skunks and porcupines. Given that, it is also called Flying Tiger. Call sounds like "hoo-hoo-hoo-hoooo."

displaying male

Look for the bare blue-and-red head

female

non-displaying male

Wild Turkey
Meleagris gallopavo

Size: 36–48" (91–122 cm)

Male: A large brown-and-bronze bird with a naked blue-and-red head. Long, straight black beard in the center of chest. Tail spreads open like a fan. Spurs on legs.

Female: thinner and less striking than the male; often lacks a breast beard

Juvenile: same as adult of the same sex

Nest: ground; female builds; 1 brood per year

Eggs: 10–12; buff-white with dull brown markings

When Seen: year-round

Food: insects, seeds, fruit

Compare: This bird is quite distinctive and unlikely to be confused with any other.

Stan's Notes: The largest native game bird in the Northeast, and the species from which the domestic turkey was bred. A strong flier that can approach 60 mph (97 kph). Can fly straight up, then away. Eyesight is three times better than ours. Hearing is also excellent; can hear competing males up to a mile away. Male has a "harem" of up to 20 females. Female scrapes out a shallow depression for nesting and pads it with soft leaves. Males are known as toms, females are hens, young are poults. Roosts in trees at night. It was eliminated from many states in the Northeast due to market hunting and loss of habitat, and reintroduced during the 1960–70s. Populations are now stable.

male

*Look for the
rusty-red chest*

female

Red-breasted Nuthatch
Sitta canadensis

Size: 4½" (11 cm)

Male: Gray-backed bird with an obvious black eye line and black cap. Rust-red breast and belly.

Female: duller than the male and has a gray cap and pale undersides

Juvenile: same as female

Nest: cavity; male and female excavate a cavity or move into a vacant hole; 1 brood per year

Eggs: 5–6; white with red-brown markings

When Seen: year-round

Food: insects, insect eggs, seeds; comes to seed and suet feeders

Compare: White-breasted Nuthatch (pg. 131) is larger and has a white breast. Look for the rust-red breast and black eye line to help identify the Red-breasted Nuthatch.

Stan's Notes: The nuthatch climbs down trunks of trees headfirst, searching for insects. Like a chickadee, it grabs a seed from a feeder and flies off to crack it open. Wedges the seed into a crevice and pounds it open with several sharp blows. The name "Nuthatch" comes from the Middle English moniker *nuthak,* referring to the habit of hacking seeds open. Look for it in mature conifers, where it extracts seeds from pine cones. Excavates a cavity or takes an old woodpecker hole or a natural cavity and builds a nest within. An irruptive migrator, common in some winters and scarce in others. Gives a series of nasal "yank-yank-yank" calls.

Look for the black cap

Black-capped Chickadee
Poecile atricapillus

Size: 5" (13 cm)

Male: Familiar gray bird with a black cap and throat patch. Tan sides and belly. White chest. Small white wing marks.

Female: same as male

Juvenile: same as adult

Nest: cavity; female and male excavate or use a nest box; 1 brood per year

Eggs: 5–7; white with fine brown markings

When Seen: year-round

Food: seeds, insects, fruit; will come to seed and suet feeders

Compare: The Tufted Titmouse (pg. 135) is larger and has a crest.

Stan's Notes: A perky backyard bird that can be attracted with a nest box or bird feeder. Usually the first to find a new seed or suet feeder. Can be easily tamed and hand fed. Much of the diet comes from bird feeders, so it can be a common urban bird. Needs to feed every day in winter and forages to find food even during the worst winter storms. Typically seen with nuthatches, woodpeckers and other birds. Builds nest mostly with green moss and lines it with fur. Named "Chickadee" for its familiar "chika-dee-dee-dee-dee" call. Also gives a high-pitched, two-toned "fee-bee" call. Can have different calls in different regions.

male

Look for the
white chest

female

White-breasted Nuthatch

Sitta carolinensis

Size: 5–6" (13–15 cm)

Male: Slate-gray with a white face, breast and belly, and a large white patch on the rump. Black cap and nape of neck. Bill is long and thin, slightly upturned. Chestnut undertail.

Female: similar to male, but has a gray cap and nape

Juvenile: similar to female

Nest: cavity; female and male build a nest within; 1 brood per year

Eggs: 5–7; white with brown markings

When Seen: year-round

Food: insects, insect eggs, seeds; comes to seed and suet feeders

Compare: Red-breasted Nuthatch (pg. 127) is smaller and has a rust-red belly and distinctive black eye line. Look for the white breast to help identify the White-breasted Nuthatch.

Stan's Notes: The nuthatch hops headfirst down trees, looking for insects that birds climbing up miss. Its climbing agility is due to an extra-long hind toe claw, or nail, that is nearly twice the size of its front claws. "Nuthatch," from the Middle English *nuthak,* refers to the bird's habit of wedging a seed in a crevice and hacking it open. Often seen in flocks with chickadees, Brown Creepers and Downy Woodpeckers. Mates stay together year-round, defending a small territory. Gives a characteristic "whi-whi-whi-whi" spring call during February and March.

Look for the
pink bill

female
pg. 87

male

Dark-eyed Junco
Junco hyemalis

Size: 5½" (14 cm)

Male: A plump, dark-eyed bird with a slate-gray-to-charcoal chest, head and back. White belly. Pink bill. White outer tail feathers appear like a white V in flight.

Female: round bird with brown plumage

Juvenile: similar to female, with streaking on the breast and head

Nest: cup; female and male build; 2 broods per year

Eggs: 3–5; white with reddish-brown markings

When Seen: fall to winter; year-round in some areas

Food: seeds, insects; visits ground and seed feeders

Compare: Rarely confused with any other bird. Look for the pink bill and small flocks feeding under feeders to identify the male Dark-eyed Junco.

Stan's Notes: One of the most common winter birds in the region. Migrates from Canada and northern parts of Minnesota to areas farther south. Adheres to a rigid social hierarchy, with dominant birds chasing the less dominant birds. Look for the white outer tail feathers flashing in flight. Often seen in small flocks on the ground, where it uses its feet to simultaneously "double-scratch" to expose seeds and insects. Eats many weed seeds. Nests in a wide variety of wooded habitats. Several subspecies of Dark-eyed Junco were previously considered to be separate species.

*Look for the
pointed crest*

Tufted Titmouse

Baeolophus bicolor

Size: 6" (15 cm)

Male: Slate-gray bird with a white chest and belly. Pointed crest. Rust-brown wash on the flanks. Gray legs and dark eyes.

Female: same as male

Juvenile: same as adult

Nest: cavity; female lines an old woodpecker cavity; 2 broods per year

Eggs: 5–7; white with brown markings

When Seen: year-round

Food: insects, seeds, fruit; will come to seed and suet feeders

Compare: Black-capped Chickadee (pg. 129) is a close relative, but it is smaller and lacks a crest. The White-breasted Nuthatch (pg. 131) has a rust-brown undertail. Look for the pointed crest to help identify the Tufted Titmouse.

Stan's Notes: A common feeder bird that can be attracted with an offering of black oil sunflower seeds or suet. Can also be attracted with a nest box. Well known for its "peter-peter-peter" call, which it quickly repeats. Notorious for pulling hair from sleeping dogs, cats and squirrels to line its nest. Usually seen only one or two at a time. Male feeds the female during courtship and nesting. The prefix "tit" in the common name comes from a Scandinavian word meaning "little." Suffix "mouse" is derived from the Old English word *mase*, meaning "bird." Simply translated, it is a "small bird."

Look for the tail pumping while perching

Eastern Phoebe
Sayornis phoebe

Size: 7" (18 cm)

Male: Plain gray bird with slightly darker wings, a light olive-green belly and thin dark bill.

Female: same as male

Juvenile: same as adult

Nest: cup; female builds; 2 broods per year

Eggs: 4–5; white without markings

When Seen: spring and summer

Food: insects

Compare: Gray Catbird (pg. 139) has a black crown and a chestnut patch under its tail. The Eastern Phoebe lacks any distinctive markings. Listen for its well-enunciated "fee-bee" call and look for the hawking and tail-pumping behaviors to help identify this bird.

Stan's Notes: A sparrow-sized bird that often perches on the end of a dead branch. Found in forests, yards and farms. In a process called hawking, it waits for a passing insect. When a bug flies near, it launches out to catch it and then returns to the same branch. It has a very distinctive habit of pumping its tail up and down while perching. Builds a nest beneath the eaves of a house, under a bridge or in another sheltered spot. Uses mud, grass and moss for nest materials and hair (and sometimes feathers) for the lining. The common name is derived from its very distinctive "fee-bee" call, which it repeats over and over from the top of dead branches.

Look for the black crown

Gray Catbird
Dumetella carolinensis

Size: 9" (23 cm)

Male: Handsome slate-gray bird with a black crown and a long, thin black bill. Often lifts up its tail, exposing a chestnut patch beneath.

Female: same as male

Juvenile: same as adult

Nest: cup; female and male build; 2 broods per year

Eggs: 4–6; blue-green without markings

When Seen: spring, summer and fall

Food: insects, occasional fruit; visits suet feeders

Compare: Eastern Phoebe (pg. 137) is smaller and has an olive belly. To help identify the Gray Catbird, look for the black crown and a chestnut patch under the tail.

Stan's Notes: A secretive bird, more often heard than seen. The Chippewa Indians gave it a name that means "the bird that cries with grief" due to its raspy call. Called "Catbird" because the sound is like the meowing of a house cat. Often mimics other birds, rarely repeating the same phrases. Found in forest edges, backyards and parks. Builds its nest with small twigs. Nests in thick shrubs and quickly flies back into shrubs if approached. If a cowbird lays an egg in its nest, the catbird will quickly break it and eject it.

male

Look for the rusty-red breast

female

American Robin

Turdus migratorius

Size: 9–11" (23–28 cm)

Male: Familiar gray bird with a dark rust-red breast and a nearly black head and tail. White chin with black streaks. White eye-ring.

Female: similar to male, with a duller rust-red breast and gray head

Juvenile: similar to female, with a speckled breast and brown back

Nest: cup; female builds with help from the male; 2–3 broods per year

Eggs: 4–7; pale blue without markings

When Seen: spring through fall, some stay all winter

Food: insects, fruit, berries, earthworms

Compare: Familiar bird to all. To differentiate the male from the female, compare the nearly black head and rust-red chest of the male with the gray head and duller chest of the female.

Stan's Notes: Can be heard singing all night in spring. City robins sing louder than country robins in order to hear each other over traffic and noise. A robin isn't listening for worms when it turns its head to one side. It is focusing its sight out of one eye to look for dirt moving, which is caused by worms moving. Territorial, often fighting its reflection in a window. Some robins stay in low, swampy areas during winter, feeding on leftover berries and insect eggs. Some of these non-migrators will die before spring.

Look for the white wing patches

displaying

Northern Mockingbird

Mimus polyglottos

Size: 10" (25 cm)

Male: Silvery-gray head and back with a light-gray breast and belly. White wing patches, seen in flight or during display. Tail mostly black with white outer tail feathers. Black bill.

Female: same as male

Juvenile: dull gray with a heavily streaked breast and a gray bill

Nest: cup; female and male construct; 2 broods per year, sometimes more

Eggs: 3–5; blue-green with brown markings

When Seen: year-round in many places

Food: insects, fruit

Compare: The Gray Catbird (pg. 139) is slate gray and lacks wing patches. Look for the Mockingbird to spread its wings, flash its white wing patches and wag its tail from side to side.

Stan's Notes: A very animated bird. Performs an elaborate mating dance. Facing each other with heads and tails erect, pairs will run toward each other, flashing their white wing patches, and then retreat to cover nearby. Thought to flash the wing patches to scare up insects when hunting. Sits for long periods on top of shrubs. Imitates other birds (vocal mimicry); hence the common name. Young males often sing at night. Often unafraid of people, allowing for close observation.

juvenile

soaring

*Look for
the banded,
squared tip
of the tail*

Sharp-shinned Hawk

Accipiter striatus

Size:	10–14" (25–36 cm); up to 2' wingspan
Male:	Small woodland hawk with a gray back and head and rust-red chest. Short wings. A long, squared tail and several dark tail bands, with the widest band at the end of tail. Red eyes.
Female:	same as male, only larger
Juvenile:	same size as adults, with a brown back, heavy streaking on the chest and yellow eyes
Nest:	platform; female builds; 1 brood per year
Eggs:	4–5; white with brown markings
When Seen:	year-round
Food:	birds, small mammals
Compare:	Cooper's Hawk (pg. 149) is much larger and has a larger head, a slightly longer neck and rounded tail. Look for the squared tail to help identify Sharp-shinned Hawk.

Stan's Notes: A common hawk of backyards, parks and woodlands. Constructs its nest with sticks, usually high in a tree. Typically seen swooping in on birds visiting feeders and chasing them as they flee. Its short wingspan and long tail help it to maneuver through thick stands of trees in pursuit of prey. Calls a loud, high-pitched "kik-kik-kik-kik." Named "Sharp-shinned" for the sharp projection (keel) on the leading edge of its shin. A bird's shin is actually below the ankle (rather than above it, like ours) on the tarsus bone of its foot. In most birds, the tarsus bone is round, not sharp.

*Look for
the gleaming,
iridescent patches*

Rock Pigeon
Columba livia

Size:	13" (33 cm)
Male:	No set color pattern. Shades of gray-to-white with patches of gleaming, iridescent green and blue. Often has a light rump patch.
Female:	same as male
Juvenile:	same as adult
Nest:	platform; female builds; 3–4 broods per year
Eggs:	1–2; white without markings
When Seen:	year-round
Food:	seeds, fruit; visits ground and seed feeders
Compare:	Mourning Dove (pg. 119) is smaller, light brown and lacks the variety of color combinations of the Rock Pigeon.

Stan's Notes: Also known as Domestic Pigeon. Formerly known as Rock Dove. Introduced to North America from Europe by the early settlers. Most common around cities and barnyards, where it scratches for seeds. One of the few birds with a wide variety of colors, produced by years of selective breeding while in captivity. Parents feed the young a regurgitated liquid known as crop-milk for the first few days of life. One of the few birds that can drink without tilting its head back. Nests under bridges or on buildings, balconies, barns and sheds. Was once thought to be a nuisance in cities and was poisoned. Now, many cities have Peregrine Falcons (not shown) feeding on Rock Pigeons, which keeps their numbers in check.

soaring

juvenile

*Look for
the banded,
rounded tip
of the tail*

Cooper's Hawk
Accipiter cooperii

Size: 14–20" (36–51 cm); up to 3' wingspan

Male: Medium-sized hawk with short wings and a long, rounded tail with several black bands. Slate-gray back, rusty breast, dark wing tips. Gray bill with a bright yellow spot at the base. Dark red eyes.

Female: similar to male, only larger

Juvenile: brown back, brown streaking on the breast, bright yellow eyes

Nest: platform; male and female construct; 1 brood per year

Eggs: 2–4; greenish with brown markings

When Seen: year-round

Food: small birds, mammals

Compare: The Sharp-shinned Hawk (pg. 145) is much smaller, lighter gray and has a squared tail. Look for the banded, rounded tail to help identify the Cooper's Hawk.

Stan's Notes: Found in many habitats, from woodlands to parks and backyards. Stubby wings help it to navigate around trees while it chases small birds. Will ambush prey, flying into heavy brush or even running on the ground in pursuit. Comes to feeders, hunting for birds. Flies with long glides followed by a few quick flaps. Calls a loud, clear "cack-cack-cack-cack." The young have gray eyes that turn bright yellow at 1 year and turn dark red later, after 3–5 years.

male

Look for
the gleaming,
ruby-red throat

female

Ruby-throated Hummingbird
Archilochus colubris

Size: 3–3½" (7.5–9 cm)

Male: Tiny iridescent green bird. Black throat patch reflects bright ruby-red in direct sunlight.

Female: same as male, but lacks a throat patch

Juvenile: same as female

Nest: cup; female builds; 1–2 broods per year

Eggs: 2; white without markings

When Seen: summer

Food: nectar, insects; will come to nectar feeders

Compare: No other bird is as tiny. The Sphinx Moth also hovers at flowers, but it has clear wings, doesn't hum in flight, moves much slower than the Ruby-throat and can be approached.

Stan's Notes: This is the smallest bird in the Northeast. Can fly straight up, straight down, backward, or hover in midair. Does not sing but will chatter or buzz to communicate. Weighing about the same as a U.S. penny, it takes about five average-sized hummingbirds to equal the weight of one chickadee. The wings create the humming sound. Flaps 50–60 times or more per second when flying at top speed. Breathes 250 times per minute. Heart beats 1,260 times per minute. Builds a stretchy nest with plant material and spiderwebs, gluing pieces of lichen to the exterior for camouflage. Attracted to colorful tubular flowers. Will extract and eat insects trapped in spiderwebs. A long-distance migrator, wintering in the tropics of Central America.

Look for the black head

male

female
pg. 165

Baltimore Oriole

Icterus galbula

Size: 7–8" (18–20 cm)

Male: Flaming orange oriole with a black head and back. White-and-orange wing bars. Orange-and-black tail. Gray bill and dark eyes.

Female: pale yellow with orange tones, gray-brown wings, white wing bars, gray bill, dark eyes

Juvenile: same as female

Nest: pendulous; female builds; 1 brood per year

Eggs: 4–5; bluish with brown markings

When Seen: spring and summer

Food: insects, fruit, nectar; comes to nectar, orange half and grape jelly feeders

Compare: Male Orchard Oriole (pg. 155) is much darker orange. Look for the flaming orange to identify the male Baltimore Oriole.

Stan's Notes: A fantastic songster, often heard before seen. Easily attracted to a bird feeder that offers sugar water (nectar), orange halves or grape jelly. Parents bring their young to feeders. Sits at the top of trees, feeding on caterpillars. Female builds a sock-like nest at the outermost branches of tall trees. Prefers parks, yards and forests and often returns to the same area year after year. Seen during migration and summer. Some of the last birds to arrive in spring (May) and first to leave in the fall (September). Young males turn orange-and-black at 1½ years of age.

Look for the
black head and throat

male

first-year male

female
pg. 167

Orchard Oriole

Icterus spurius

Size: 7–8" (18–20 cm)

Male: Dark orange oriole with a black head, throat, upper back, wings and tail. White wing bar. Bill is long and thin. Gray mark on lower bill.

Female: olive-green back, dull yellow belly and gray wings with two indistinct white wing bars

Juvenile: same as female; first-year male looks like the female with a black bib

Nest: pendulous; female builds; 1 brood per year

Eggs: 3–5; pale blue-to-white, brown markings

When Seen: spring and summer

Food: insects, fruit, nectar; comes to nectar, orange half and grape jelly feeders

Compare: The male Baltimore Oriole (pg. 153) is brighter orange. Look for the dark orange plumage to identify the male Orchard Oriole.

Stan's Notes: Named "Orchard" for its preference for orchards. Also likes open woods. Eats insects until wild fruit starts to ripen. Often nests alone; sometimes nests in small colonies. Parents bring their young to bird feeding stations after they fledge. Many people don't see these birds at their feeders very much during the summer and think they have left, but the birds are still there, hunting for insects to feed to their young. Some of the first birds to migrate at the end of summer. Often migrates in flocks with Baltimore Orioles.

Look for the reddish face and the brown cap

male

female
pg. 79

yellow
male

House Finch
Haemorhous mexicanus

Size: 5" (13 cm)

Male: Small finch with a red-to-orange face, throat, chest and rump. Brown cap. Brown marking behind eyes. White belly with brown streaks. Brown wings with white streaks.

Female: brown with a heavily streaked white chest

Juvenile: similar to female

Nest: cup, occasionally in a cavity, female builds; 2 broods per year

Eggs: 4–5; pale blue, lightly marked

When Seen: year-round

Food: seeds, fruit, leaf buds; visits seed feeders and feeders that offer grape jelly

Compare: Male Purple Finch (pg. 159) has a red cap. Look for the brown cap and streaked belly to help identify the male House Finch.

Stan's Notes: Can be a common bird at your feeders. A very social bird, visiting feeders in small flocks. Likes to nest in hanging flower baskets. Male sings a loud, cheerful warbling song. It was originally introduced to Long Island, New York, from the western U.S. in the 1940s. Now found throughout the country. Suffers from a disease that causes the eyes to crust, resulting in blindness and death. Rarely, some males are yellow (see inset), perhaps due to poor diet.

Look for the raspberry-red cap

male

female
pg. 93

Purple Finch
Haemorhous purpureus

Size:	6" (15 cm)
Male:	Raspberry-red head, cap, chest, back and rump. Brownish wings and tail. Large bill.
Female:	heavily streaked brown-and-white bird with bold white eyebrows
Juvenile:	same as female
Nest:	cup; female and male build; 1 brood per year
Eggs:	4–5; greenish-blue with brown markings
When Seen:	year-round
Food:	seeds, insects, fruit; comes to seed feeders
Compare:	The male House Finch (pg. 157) has a brown cap and a streaked belly. Look for the raspberry-red cap to help identify the male Purple Finch.

Stan's Notes: An irruptive migrator, seen in the Northeast at different times of the year but not always here every winter. Travels in flocks of up to 50 birds. Visits seed feeders along with House Finches, which makes it hard to tell them apart. Ash tree seeds are an important source of food; feeds mainly on seeds. Found in coniferous forests, mixed woods, woodland edges and suburban backyards. Flies in the typical undulating, up-and-down pattern of finches. Sings a rich, loud song. Gives a distinctive "tic" note only in flight. Male is not purple. The Latin species name *purpureus* means "purple" or other reddish colors.

female
pg. 109

male

Look for the
black mask

juvenile

Northern Cardinal
Cardinalis cardinalis

Size: 8–9" (20–23 cm)

Male: Red bird with a black mask that extends from the face to the throat. Large crest and large red bill.

Female: buff-brown with a black mask, large reddish bill and red tinges on the crest and wings

Juvenile: same as female, but with a blackish-gray bill

Nest: cup; female builds; 2–3 broods per year

Eggs: 3–4; bluish-white with brown markings

When Seen: year-round

Food: seeds, insects, fruit; comes to seed feeders

Compare: Once you recognize its bright coloration and large bill, there aren't many birds to mistake for the cardinal.

Stan's Notes: A familiar backyard bird. Seen in a variety of habitats, including parks. Usually likes thick vegetation. One of the few species in which both males and females sing. Can be heard all year. Listen for its "whata-cheer-cheer-cheer" territorial call in spring. Watch for a male feeding a female during courtship. The male also feeds the young of the first brood while the female builds a second nest. Territorial in spring, fighting its own reflection in a window or other reflective surface. Non-territorial in winter, gathering in small flocks of up to 20 birds. Makes short flights from cover, often landing on the ground. *Cardinalis* denotes importance, as represented by the red garments of Catholic cardinals.

Look for the black forehead

winter male

male

female

American Goldfinch

Spinus tristis

Size: 5" (13 cm)

Male: Bright canary-yellow finch with a black forehead and tail. Black wings with white wing bars. White rump. No markings on the chest. Winter male is similar to the female.

Female: dull olive-yellow plumage with brown wings; lacks a black forehead

Juvenile: same as female

Nest: cup; female builds; 1 brood per year

Eggs: 4–6; pale blue without markings

When Seen: year-round

Food: seeds, insects; comes to seed feeders

Compare: The Pine Siskin (pg. 77) has a streaked chest and belly and yellow wing bars. The female House Finch (pg. 79) and Purple Finch (pg. 93) have heavily streaked chests.

Stan's Notes: A common backyard resident. Most often found in open fields, scrubby areas and woodlands. Enjoys Nyjer seed in feeders. Breeds in late summer. Lines its nest with the silky down from wild thistle. Almost always in small flocks. Twitters while it flies. Flight is roller coaster-like. Moves around to find adequate food during winter. Often called Wild Canary due to the male's canary-colored plumage. Male sings a pleasant, high-pitched song.

Look for the gray-brown wings

female

male
pg. 153

Baltimore Oriole

Icterus galbula

Size: 7–8" (18–20 cm)

Female: A pale yellow oriole with orange tones, gray-brown wings and white wing bars. Gray bill. Dark eyes.

Male: flaming orange with a black head and back, white-and-orange wing bars, an orange-and-black tail, gray bill and dark eyes

Juvenile: same as female

Nest: pendulous; female builds; 1 brood per year

Eggs: 4–5; bluish with brown markings

When Seen: spring and summer

Food: insects, fruit, nectar; comes to nectar, orange half and grape jelly feeders

Compare: Female Orchard Oriole (pg. 167) has a dull yellow belly. Look for the gray-brown wings to help identify the female Baltimore Oriole.

Stan's Notes: A fantastic songster, often heard before seen. Easily attracted to a bird feeder that offers sugar water (nectar), orange halves or grape jelly. Parents bring their young to feeders. Sits at the top of trees, feeding on caterpillars. Female builds a sock-like nest at the outermost branches of tall trees. Prefers parks, yards and forests and often returns to the same area year after year. Seen during migration and summer. Some of the last birds to arrive in spring (May) and first to leave in the fall (September). Young males turn orange-and-black at 1½ years of age.

male
pg. 155

Look for the
dull yellow belly

female

first-year male

Orchard Oriole

Icterus spurius

Size: 7–8" (18–20 cm)

Female: An olive-green oriole with a dull yellow belly. Gray wings with two indistinct white wing bars. Bill is long and thin, with a gray mark on the lower bill (mandible).

Male: dark orange with a black head, throat, upper back, wings and tail, one white wing bar

Juvenile: same as female; first-year male looks like the female with a black bib

Nest: pendulous; female builds; 1 brood per year

Eggs: 3–5; pale blue-to-white, brown markings

When Seen: spring and summer

Food: insects, fruit, nectar; comes to nectar, orange half and grape jelly feeders

Compare: Female Baltimore Oriole (pg. 165) has orange tones and more-distinct wing bars.

Stan's Notes: Named "Orchard" for its preference for orchards. Also likes open woods. Eats insects until wild fruit starts to ripen. Often nests alone; sometimes nests in small colonies. Parents bring their young to bird feeding stations after they fledge. Many people don't see these birds at their feeders very much during the summer and think they have left, but the birds are still there, hunting for insects to feed to their young. Some of the first birds to migrate at the end of summer. Often migrates in flocks with Baltimore Orioles.

Birding on the Internet

Birding online is a great way to discover additional information and learn more about birds. These websites will assist you in your pursuit of birds. Web addresses sometimes change a bit, so if one no longer works, just enter the name of the group into a search engine to track down the new address.

Author Stan Tekiela's homepage

naturesmart.com

American Birding Association

aba.org

The Cornell Lab of Ornithology

birds.cornell.edu

eBird

ebird.org

Christmas Bird Count

www.audubon.org/conservation/science/christmas-bird-count

Great Backyard Bird Count

gbbc.birdcount.org

Feather Atlas

www.fws.gov/lab/featheratlas

Zooniverse

www.zooniverse.org
(several citizen science projects pertaining to birds)

Checklist/Index by Species

Use the boxes to check the birds you've seen.

Glossary

birdsong: A series of musical notes that a bird strings together in a pleasing melody. Also called a song.

brood: A family of related bird siblings that hatched at around the same time.

brood parasites: Birds that don't nest, incubate or raise families, such as Brown-headed Cowbirds (pp. 41 and 101). See *host*.

call: A nonmusical sound, often a single note, that is repeated.

carrion: A dead and often rotting animal's body, or carcass, that is an important food for many other animals, including birds.

citizen science: Science projects that harness data from the observations of everyday people; the Christmas Backyard Bird Count and the Great Backyard Bird Count are examples.

colony: A group of birds nesting together in the same area. The size of a colony can range from two pairs to hundreds of birds.

coniferous: A tree or shrub that has evergreen, needle-like leaves and that produces cones.

cover: A dense area of trees or shrubs where birds nest or hide.

crop-milk: A liquid that pigeons and doves regurgitate (spit up) to feed their young.

deciduous: A tree or shrub that sheds its leaves every year.

display: An attention-getting behavior of birds to impress and attract a mate, or to draw predators away from the nest. A display may include dramatic movements in flight or on the ground.

dimorphic: Bird species in which the males and females look different (the Northern Cardinal, pp. 109 and 161 is an example).

excavate: To dig or carefully remove wood or dirt, creating a cavity, hole or tunnel.

fledge: The process of developing flight feathers and leaving the nest.

flock: A group of the same bird species or a gathering of mixed species of birds. Flocks range from a pair of birds to upwards of 10,000 individuals.

habitat: The natural home or environment of a bird.

hatchlings: Baby birds that have recently emerged from their eggs. See *nestlings*.

hood: The markings on the head of a bird, resembling a hood.

horns: A tuft or collection of feathers, usually on top of a bird's head, resembling horns.

host: A bird species that takes care of the eggs and babies of other bird species. See *brood parasites*.

incubation: The process of sitting on bird eggs in the nest to keep them warm until they hatch.

iridescent: A luminous, or bright, quality of feathers, with colors seeming to change when viewed from different angles.

irruptive migrator: A bird that migrates irregularly and suddenly.

juvenile: A bird that isn't an adult yet.

lore: The area on each side of a bird's face between the eye and the base of the bill.

migrate: The regular, predictable pattern of seasonal movement by some birds from one region to another, especially to escape winter.

molt: The process of dropping old, worn-out feathers and replacing them with new feathers, usually only one feather at a time.

necklace: The markings around the neck of a bird, as seen in the Killdeer (pg. 113).

nape: The back of a bird's neck.

nectar: A sugar and water solution found in plant flowers.

nestlings: Young birds that have not yet left the nest. See *hatchlings*.

plumage: The collective set of feathers on a bird at any given time.

prey: Any critter that is hunted and killed by another for food.

raptor: A flesh-eating bird of prey that hunts and kills for food. Hawks, eagles, ospreys, falcons, owls and vultures are raptors. See *prey*.

regurgitate: The process of bringing swallowed food up again to the mouth to feed young birds.

sublingual: Under the tongue; some bird species have anatomical adaptations that allow them to carry seeds or food under their tongue.

suet: Animal fat, usually beef, that has been heated and made into cakes to feed birds.

thermal: A column of warm air moving upwards; some birds use them when soaring.

twitter: A high-pitched call of a bird. See *call*.

undulating: In an up-and-down motion, usually referring to a bird's flight pattern.

Embrace Nature with

BIRDS

Birds of Connecticut

Birds of Maine

Birds of Maryland & Delaware

Birds of Massachusetts

Birds of New Hampshire
& Vermont

Birds of New Jersey

Birds of New York

Birds of Pennsylvania

Birds of Prey of
the Northeast

TREES

Trees of New York

Trees of Pennsylvania

POPULAR BIRD BOOKS

Birds of the Northeast
Quick Guide

Bird Migration

Bird Trivia

More from Stan Tekiela

CHILDREN'S BOOKS

Baby Bear Discovers the World
The Cutest Critter
Do Beavers Need Blankets?
Hidden Critters
Jump, Little Wood Ducks
Some Babies Are Wild
Super Animal Powers
What Eats That?
Whose Baby Butt?
Whose Butt?
Whose Track is That?

PLAYING CARDS

Birds of the Northeast
Mammals of the Northeast
Trees of the Northeast
Wildflowers of the Northeast
Hummingbirds
Loons
Owls
Raptors

About the Author

Naturalist, wildlife photographer and writer Stan Tekiela is the originator of the popular state-specific field guide series that includes *Birds of New York, Birds of Massachusetts,* and many other guides to birds and birding in the Northeast. Stan has authored more than 190 educational books, including field guides, quick guides, nature books, children's books and more, presenting many species of animals and plants.

With a Bachelor of Science degree in natural history from the University of Minnesota and as an active professional naturalist for more than 30 years, Stan studies and photographs wildlife throughout the United States and Canada. He has received national and regional awards for his books and photographs and is also a well-known columnist and radio personality. His syndicated column appears in more than 25 newspapers, and his wildlife programs are broadcast on a number of Midwest radio stations. You can follow Stan on Facebook and Twitter or contact him via his website, naturesmart.com.